Murder Play

A Play

Brian J. Burton

Samuel French—London
New York – Sydney – Toronto – Hollywood

CHARACTERS

Peter Darrell

Robyn Darrell

Jane Valentine

David Valentine

The action takes place in the living-room of Jane and David Valentine's house in Cornwall

Time—the present

MURDER PLAY

The living-room of Jane and David Valentine. Early morning

There is a fireplace with a mantelshelf in the back wall C, *with windows on each side. In front of the window* L *is a high-backed settee facing away from the audience. Below this, there is a long, low coffee table with bottles, glasses and a handbag on it. There is another settee* RC *with a small table next to it covered with dirty glasses. An armchair stands* DR *against the wall, and above this there is a record player. There is a door* DL, *up stage of which is a mirror on the wall. A full ashtray lies on the floor* C

When the CURTAIN *rises, the room is in semi-darkness. It is daylight outside but the window curtains are closed. Jane Valentine is slumped asleep in the armchair, Peter is lying full length on the settee* RC *and Robyn is curled up on the floor* C. *David Valentine is lying on the high-backed settee out of sight of the audience, apparently asleep. There is a record on the turntable of the record player, which is repeating the run-out over and over again. After a moment or two, Peter stirs, sits up and rubs his eyes*

Peter Christ! (*He looks at his watch with some difficulty*) It's eight o'clock! What the hell? (*He gets up, goes to the record player and turns it off. Then he moves to the window* R *and draws back the curtains*)

The room becomes lighter

(*Turning from the window*) Hey, you lot—wake up! It's eight o'clock. (*He pauses*) I said it was eight o'clock. Did you hear me? (*He moves to Robyn*) Robyn, come on—time to get up. The party's over. Time we went home.

Robyn (*stirring*) Who's that? What do you want? (*She opens her eyes*) Oh, it's you. What did you say? I didn't hear you properly. I was asleep.

Peter Weren't we all? I said it was eight o'clock—time we went home.

Robyn (*sitting up*) It can't be.
Peter But it is, I tell you. We must have been asleep for hours.
God, I've got a stiff neck. (*He rubs his neck*) I can't remember a
damn thing. Can you?
Robyn (*rising and going across to the mirror* L) I feel like death.
And I look like it too. (*She runs her fingers through her hair*)
God, what a sight! Where are the Valentines—have you any
idea?
Peter That looks like Jane over there in the armchair. (*He goes
across to the armchair*) She's dead to the world. (*He shakes
Jane*) Hey, Jane—come on—time to get up. (*He shakes her
again*) Jane, it's after eight o'clock. Did you hear me?
Jane (*murmuring*) Go to hell!
Peter Jane, it's time to get up. Jane, I . . .
Robyn Oh, leave her, Peter. She's more than likely to be out
cold for hours yet. She was in a fair old state, if I remember
rightly. Let her sleep it off. It's her house anyway.
Peter You weren't exactly stone cold sober yourself, were
you?
Robyn (*moving to the coffee table and collecting her handbag*)
Neither were you, if it comes to that. In fact, I don't think I
ever remember you so tipsy. (*She goes back to the mirror and
combs her hair*) I look as though I've been dragged through a
hedge backwards.
Peter You think we should leave her where she is, then?
Robyn I think it would be best, yes.
Peter O.K. As soon as you've finished your face then, we'll be
off. I'm not mad keen to stay any longer, are you?
Robyn (*applying lipstick*) No point, is there? I'll be ready in a
tick.
Peter Right. Can you see all right? I'll draw back the other
curtain. (*He goes to the window* L)
Robyn Thank you.
Peter God knows where our charming host has disappeared to.
(*He draws back the curtains*)

*The room becomes lighter. As Peter turns away from the window,
he glances at the high-backed settee*

(*Checking*) Talk of the devil!
Robyn What's up?

Peter I've found him. He's here on the settee.

Robyn Who?

Peter David.

Robyn So what?

Peter I just thought you'd like to know, that's all.

Robyn Not particularly. Leave him, Peter. He might wake up. He's the last person I want to talk to this morning.

Peter I'm with you there—one hundred per cent. (*He moves to the other settee and perches on the arm*) You know, it's incredible, it really is. To look at him lying there, sleeping like a baby, you wouldn't believe what happened last night, would you? It's like some sort of ghastly nightmare.

Robyn (*turning to face Peter*) Oh, it happened all right—it happened—no doubt about that, I can assure you.

Peter But to go about it the way he did. I find that almost . . .

Robyn Do we have to talk about it now? Leave it, Peter, please. We'll talk about it when we get home. I just want to get out of here.

Peter O.K. Suits me. (*He holds out his hands*) Come on then—let's go. (*He rises*)

Robyn (*going to him*) I'm ready. I've carried out some emergency repairs. They'll have to do till we get home.

Peter No-one will see you in the car. Anyway, you look fine.

Robyn Thank you.

Peter Did you have a coat? I can't remember.

Robyn No—only a hat. I left it on that chest thing in the hall.

Peter (*pleasantly*) You and your hats. You have to wear a hat, don't you?

Robyn Of course. I don't feel dressed without one when we go out. That's just me. Come on, then. (*She goes towards the door*)

Peter starts to follow her, then stops suddenly

Peter Do you think we ought to leave them a note or something?

Robyn What—to thank them for a pleasant evening? You have to be joking. No—come on. We might give them a ring this afternoon or something.

Peter I expect you're right. O.K. Home time. (*He moves to the door*)

Jane (*opening an eye*) Where are you two sneaking off to?

Peter (*turning back from the door*) You've returned to the land

of the living, have you? We thought you'd be asleep for a
while yet. How do you feel?
Jane Not too bad really—considering. A bit of a head and a
pretty ghastly tongue but otherwise fine. You're not going,
are you?
Peter It's getting late.
Jane Why, what time is it?
Peter Past eight.
Jane Is that all? What the hell? It's Sunday, isn't it? (*She rises
from the armchair*) Look, I'll go and make some coffee. I think
we could all do with a cup. I know I could.
Peter (*looking at Robyn*) Well, I don't know. I did rather . . .
Robyn Yes, so could I—a great idea. I'll come and give you a
hand.
Jane No, you stay where you are. I can manage. I won't be long
—just relax. I'll see if the papers have come yet.

Jane crosses in front of Peter and Robyn and exits

Peter I thought you were in a hurry to get home.
Robyn Another five minutes, more or less, won't make much
difference now, will it?
Peter I suppose not. (*He moves* c *and bends down to pick up the
ashtray*)
Robyn What are you doing?
Peter Just tidying up a bit.
Robyn I'd leave it if I was you.
Peter Just picking up this ashtray before someone kicks it over.
Robyn Please yourself. (*She puts her handbag on the coffee table,
then sits on the settee*) That's odd.
Peter What is? What's odd? (*He puts the ashtray on the mantel-
shelf*)
Robyn Did you notice that she didn't ask where David is?
Peter No, you're right—she didn't.
Robyn She just woke up, spoke to us and then went off to make
the coffee—just like that.
Peter Probably didn't see him there and thought he'd staggered
off to bed ages ago.
Robyn Yes—I expect you're right.
Peter I've a good mind to wake the bastard up and tell him just
what I think of him.

Robyn Oh,. shut up, Peter.

Peter What do you mean—shut up?

Robyn You said enough last night. Give it a rest. Let him sleep.

Peter Why are you springing to his defence all of a sudden?

Robyn I wasn't springing to his defence, as you put it. I just don't want to talk about it anymore.

Peter I think we let him off very lightly. (*He moves to the settee and sits on the arm*) We were far too polite about the whole thing, if you ask me.

Robyn Polite! You got a bit heated, I must say. I would hardly call the way you spoke to him polite.

Peter God, when I think of all we've done for him over the past five years and then for him to treat us like that with hardly more than a word of explanation.

Robyn Peter, please.

Peter No—I won't shut up. What was he when we joined his tin-pot little business? I'll tell you what he was. He was really just a dilettante trying to sell a few way-out arty books which the public didn't want to buy. With our help, it's built up into a thriving general bookshop.

Robyn Nobody's going to deny that. It was very fortunate for him that he met us when he did. He wouldn't have lasted another six months, I'm sure of that. All the same, from what he said last night, he is losing money and he has no alternative but to make some very drastic economies.

Peter I don't see how he can be losing money. It just doesn't make sense; the last few months . . .

Robyn Drop it, Peter—drop it. I'm tired. I don't want to talk about it now.

Peter All right—but just answer me one thing.

Robyn What?

Peter Hadn't you any idea this might happen?

Robyn Not a clue—honestly.

Peter To give us our marching orders—just like that; I still don't believe it.

Robyn I wasn't likely to know anything about it, was I? I was little more than a glorified tea lady but you were supposed to be his right-hand man. You must have realized the profit position.

Peter I hadn't the faintest idea. As you know, I checked the invoices and passed them to him for payment and I did most of the buying when the reps came in, but that was the limit of any financial control I had of the business.

Robyn Do you think he was telling the truth? Do you think the financial position is as bad as he makes out, or do you think he wanted to get rid of us for some reason and just used the profit business as an excuse?

Peter What other reason could there be?

Robyn I don't know. I was just asking.

Peter Business has been a bit slow lately but it's been worse than it is now, on more than one occasion, in the past. We've always got by before. (*He pauses*) I still can't get over the way he went about it—inviting us round to dinner, getting us half cut then giving us the push.

Robyn Supposing it's one of those dreadful practical jokes of his.

Peter I'd hardly think so. If it is, it's one of the sickest ones he's pulled yet. No—I'm quite certain he wasn't joking last night. He said he'd been meaning to tell us for several weeks, didn't he?

Robyn He certainly got drunk after he'd told us.

Peter He was well away before then.

Robyn Probably needed a few drinks to summon up the courage to tell us.

Peter Who—David? Don't you believe it. Don't let that ever so gentlemanly manner fool you. He's as hard as nails underneath that polished veneer.

Robyn I wouldn't say that at all. I don't think you know the real David.

Peter And you do—is that it? I doubt it very much. I doubt if anyone really knows him—even Jane. He's an enigma.

Robyn I thought she was unusually quiet. She didn't have much to say for herself, for a change.

Peter She'd been well briefed, you can be sure of that. "Keep quiet and say nothing—let me do all the talking"—or something like that.

Robyn I can't think how he came to marry her in the first place —they've little in common.

Peter Attraction of opposites, perhaps. Now, you're much more his type, aren't you.

Robyn Do you think so? I wouldn't have thought so—not particularly.
Peter (*after a pause*) Perhaps he's going to take her into the shop.
Robyn Who—Calamity Jane? Perhaps he is. He'll certainly need somebody for busy periods.
Peter That would be a laugh, that would. She knows as much about books as my left foot. She probably thinks *Roget's Thesaurus* is a rock group.
Robyn That'd make a great name. I'm surprised nobody's ever thought of it.
Peter Seriously though, can you imagine her in the shop?
Robyn No—not really.
Peter I don't see how he can possibly manage on his own.
Robyn Why didn't he just get rid of one of us—why both?
Peter (*rising and moving to the coffee table*) God knows what we're going to do. We'd better start looking in the papers—not that we're likely to find any jobs in the book trade in this part of Cornwall.
Robyn We could always go back to London, I suppose.
Peter Would you want to?
Robyn You know I wouldn't. I've been very happy here away from the rat race. I don't know if I could stand London again after five years in Cornwall.
Peter You might have to. (*He turns towards Robyn*)
Robyn Could we sue him for wrongful dismissal, do you think?
Peter Shouldn't think we'd stand an earthly. If he can prove that he can't afford to keep us on, I should think he's in the clear. I don't know much about how the law operates in these cases but I wouldn't fancy our chances.
Robyn No. (*She pauses*) She's a long time getting that coffee. Do you think I ought to go and see what's keeping her?
Peter Can do, if you like.
Robyn (*rising*) I think I will then. I'd like to get home and get a bath. (*She moves to the high-backed settee*) Sleeping beauty's still well away. That's odd.
Peter What is?
Robyn He's not snoring.
Peter Why, should he be?
Robyn He's lying on his back.

Peter Perhaps he's not one of the snoring fraternity. I don't know; I've never slept with him.
Robyn Shall I wake him up?
Peter Please yourself. I'd leave him if I was you.
Robyn I'll just give him a shake. (*She leans over the back of the high-backed settee and shakes him*) Come on, David—wake up. It's getting late. Coffee's on the way. (*She turns to Peter*) Peter —he looks sort of strange. Come and have a look.
Peter What are you on about?
Robyn He looks—well, I know it sounds silly but he looks—dead.
Peter Don't be bloody stupid.

Jane enters with a coffee-pot and three cups of coffee on a tray

Jane (*as she enters*) He is.
Robyn Is what?
Jane Dead. I killed him.
Peter You what?
Jane I killed him. (*She clears a space on the coffee table for the tray*) Here's your coffee. I couldn't remember if you took sugar so I put in one spoonful.

Jane hands cups of coffee to Robyn and Peter, who take them automatically

Peter Look, I don't think that's very funny.
Jane (*moving to the settee with her coffee*) It wasn't meant to be. Drink your coffee before it gets cold. (*She sits down*)
Peter (*putting his cup on the coffee table*) You're not serious are you, for God's sake?
Jane Of course I am. Would I joke about a thing like that?
Robyn (*putting her cup on the coffee table*) I don't believe it. I just don't believe it. Is this one of David's stupid jokes?
Jane David is dead. I've just told you—and I killed him.
Robyn God! But how, when, why?
Jane One thing at a time. Shall we start with how? I stabbed him.
Robyn But you can't have.
Jane Oh, but I did.
Robyn What did you stab him with?
Jane One of those old-fashioned hat pins—you know, the long

ones. It was remarkably simple. I read in a newspaper, years ago, about someone using a hat pin. It certainly works. He hardly murmured.

Robyn My God! When did you stab him?

Jane We're on to when now, are we? Very well, I'll tell you. (*She looks at her watch*) About an hour ago, I'd say—yes, just about an hour. You were both well away—sleeping off your over-indulgence in alcohol.

Robyn What about you?

Jane Ah, yes—you both thought I'd had a lot to drink, didn't you? In actual fact, I hardly had anything. I had to remain sober if I was going to kill him.

Peter But that's not true—you were knocking back the Scotch with the rest of us.

Jane That's what I hoped you'd think. Actually I was drinking dry ginger on it's own. It's an old trick if the host wants to remain sober. Anyway, as I was saying, you were both still sleeping it off and I'd been sitting in that armchair for ages. When I was quite certain that you weren't likely to wake up for a while, I just got up out of that chair and went across to the settee. He was lying on his back, snoring like a pig—as usual. I stabbed him with the hat pin straight through the heart. He stopped snoring, gave a little grunt and died—just like that.

Peter Then?

Jane Then I pulled out the hat pin, disposed of it and went back to that chair and pretended to be asleep until you two woke me up and spoke to me.

Robyn This is like a nightmare. Look—you're making it all up, aren't you? Tell me it isn't true. David isn't dead, is he?

Jane Oh, he's dead. Make no mistake about that.

Robyn The hat pin. What did you do with it?

Jane Oh, yes—the hat pin. I put it in your handbag.

Robyn In my handbag? (*She picks up her handbag from the coffee table and starts to search through it frantically*)

Jane I'm very surprised you didn't find it when you did your hair just now. It's at the bottom underneath those Kleenex.

Peter Look, Robyn—you're wasting your time. She's mad, I tell you. You won't find a hat pin in your bag because there isn't one. She's making it all up.

Robyn (*producing a hat pin from her bag*) Look! A hat pin! She's right.

Jane I did say so—didn't I?

Robyn (*throwing the hat pin down*) It can't be. It can't be.

Jane (*rising to kneel down and pick up the hat pin by its point with her handkerchief*) People's exhibit number one. (*She wraps the hat pin in her handkerchief very carefully, then rises and crosses to the door*) Just going to put this in a safe place. I'll be back in a minute. Don't go away, will you?

Peter (*following her to the door*) Where are you going with that?

Jane exits

What in Christ's name are you up to? Come back here at once.

Jane (*off*) Back in a minute, I said.

Robyn (*moving slowly, as if in a trance, to the settee and flopping down*) This isn't happening. It's all a bad joke—don't you see? (*She pauses*) Why don't you laugh? Peter, why don't you laugh? (*She starts to laugh hysterically*)

Peter (*moving quickly towards her*) Robyn! Stop it! Pull yourself together. That doesn't help at all.

Robyn continues to laugh

Robyn, stop it—stop it!

Robyn Oh, Peter, Peter! (*She starts to cry*)

Peter That's better—that's better. (*He sits on the settee beside her and puts his arm around her*) It's all right, love. It's all right. Don't upset yourself so—please, please. There has to be some explanation. Leave it to me. love. I'll force the truth out of her when she gets back. I will, I promise. Everything's going to be O.K.—you'll see. Trust me, eh?

Robyn (*through her tears*) The hat pin—why did she put the hat pin my bag? Why on earth would she do that?

Peter I don't know. I just don't know.

Robyn And what did she mean by "people's exhibit number one"?

Peter Look, Robyn, I don't know—I really don't. All we can do is to wait till she gets back and ask her. Just leave everything to me.

Robyn Peter.

Peter What, love?

Robyn There's something you don't know—something I must tell you.

Peter Yes—what is it?

Robyn I don't know how to begin. You see . . .

Jane enters

Jane Right—that which had to be done having been done, I think it's explanation time, don't you?

Peter (*rising*) Look, this isn't some stupid party game, you know. Are you out of your mind? Look at the state Robyn's in. What the hell is this all about?

Jane I just said I'd explain, didn't I. As for Robyn, she has a very good reason to be upset.

Peter Of course she has—we all have—don't be so bloody stupid.

Jane Ah, but I didn't quite mean it like that. What I meant was that perhaps the reason she's upset isn't exactly what you imagine it is.

Peter Stop talking in riddles. What do you mean?

Jane Why don't you ask her? I said "Why don't you ask her?" Go on—ask her!

Peter I don't see . . .

Jane Or would you rather I told you?

Peter Told me what, for God's sake?

Jane Why little Miss Innocent there has been getting into such a state.

Peter (*to Robyn*) What does she mean?

There is a pause

Robyn, please—I'm asking you a question. Do you hear me?

Robyn Leave me alone—both of you. I don't want to talk about it now.

Jane Very well. I'll have to tell Peter myself then.

Robyn (*rising*) Jane! No—not now, please.

Peter (*to Robyn*) What is all this?

Jane Your dear, darling wife's been having an affair with David.

Peter No!

Jane And now David is dead and your wife, somewhat understandably, is rather upset.

Peter (*to Jane*) That's a pack of lies—isn't it? Come on—admit it.

Robyn No, Peter—she's telling the truth. I'm sorry you had to find out like this. I was going to tell you—I really was, but not now—not now.

Peter (*to Robyn*) How long has this been going on?

Robyn (*quietly*) Peter, please—can't we talk about this when we get home? I'll tell you everything then—I promise.

Peter What the hell difference does it make when you tell me? Jane seems to know all about it anyway.

Robyn It's over, Peter. I know David's dead, I don't mean that. It was over anyvay.

Peter Since when?

Robyn Yesterday. It was a day of reckoning for David in more ways than one. In the morning, he told us it was finished— he and I, I mean—and last night he gave us notice—and now he's dead. (*She starts to cry*)

Peter (*putting his arm around Robyn*) All right—let's leave it at that for now. Tell me when we get home, if you want to.

Jane Yes, I think it's time you went home. (*She moves to the coffee table and feels the coffee-pot*) The damn coffee's cold now, anyway.

Peter (*turning to Jane*) It's incredible—it really is—incredible. Five minutes ago, you stood there and calmly told us you'd killed your husband. You told us as though you were recalling some minor incident or the other—and now you tell us to go home—just like that. He's lying over there dead and you killed him. Don't you realize what you've done?

Jane Oh, yes—I realize well enough but it seems to me that there's very little you can do here now, is there?

Peter You mean you'd let us go without another word?

Jane Let you go? Of course—why not?

Peter Aren't you afraid we might go to the police?

Jane You wouldn't do that.

Robyn Why wouldn't we?

Jane There's a very good reason. Would you like me to tell you what it is?

Peter Go on.

Jane When I told you I'd killed David, you asked me how, when and why, didn't you, Robyn?

Robyn Yes.

Jane I've told you how and when—I think this might be **the**

opportune moment to tell you why. I'd sit down if I was you. It might take some time.

Peter A minute or two ago, you were telling us to go home, now you're asking us to sit down. Supposing we'd have gone just now without suggesting we might go to the police, what would you have done then?

Jane I knew you wouldn't go without finding out why I killed David. I was certain of that. I really would sit down.

Peter Oh, very well.

Peter sits Robyn on the settee and sits down beside her

Jane That's better. Very well then—you've worked with David for a number of years, haven't you? You know what a stickler for detail he was and what an amazing memory he had.

Peter It was a gift. A number of people have it. It's a sort of total recall.

Jane Oh, yes—he had a good memory—better than average, I won't deny that, but it wasn't the complete reason. He kept an elaborate diary—one of those with two pages for each day. You know the kind I mean?

Peter I think so.

Jane In that diary, he entered not only every detail of what went on in the shop but also the most intimate account of his private life. Oh, yes—a most intimate account.

Peter How do you know all this? Did he let you read it?

Jane I didn't need to read it. He read it aloud to me.

Robyn What?

Jane Every sentence, every word. Reading that diary to me was the greatest pleasure of his life.

Robyn He didn't write down the—the . . . ?

Jane The details of his little affair with you—is that what you're trying to say?

Robyn Did he?

Jane Oh, yes—it was all there—everything. Reading aloud to me the intimate details of that grubby little affair gave him enormous satisfaction.

Robyn How could he?

Jane Because that was the sort of man he was. (*She turns away*)

Robyn What do you mean?

Jane There's an old clichè about it taking all sorts to make a

world. Whatever turns you on, I guess. His satisfaction came
not only from having a string of sordid little affairs but in re-
cording his sexual adventures in a very explicit manner. But his
greatest thrill—indeed his ultimate satisfaction—came from
reading them to me.

Peter God—that's horrible—horrible. And you loved a man
like that?

Jane (*turning to them*) Loved him? I loathed him. That's why I
killed him.

Peter God!

Jane I just couldn't bear it for one more day.

Robyn But you didn't have to listen to him, did you? You could
have refused.

Jane You may have gone to bed with him but you really didn't
know him at all, did you? You didn't refuse David anything—
not a damn thing or your life wouldn't be worth living.

Robyn He was never like that with me. He was gentle and kind.

Jane Weren't you the lucky one? You weren't married to him
though, were you?

Peter I don't see what all this has to do with us not going to the
police. Whatever he did to you—vile as it was—you had no
right to take his life.

Jane You're entitled to think any way you please. You won't go
to the police though. I'm certain of that.

Peter Why won't we?

Jane (*after a pause*) I said he entered everything in that diary,
didn't I?

Peter Well?

Jane At the end of each day's entry, he left space to list all the
things he had to do the next day. The entry for the day before
yesterday included one or two trivial things which are neither
here nor there—they don't concern you. But two of the items
do concern you—very much. Number one—"Tell Robyn it's
finished."

Robyn Just like that?

Jane His exact words. Number two—"When Peter and Robyn
come to dinner, tell them they have to go"—or words to that
effect.

Peter Why should those entries prevent us from going to the
police? I don't see . . .

Jane Don't you? I'll tell you, then. In spite of his somewhat unorthodox sex life, there is not one word in that diary which even hints that he and I were not on the very best possible terms. On the contrary, there are several suggestions that I enjoyed the whole thing every bit as much as he did. I know that sounds kinky—indeed it would be if it was true—but he makes the point repeatedly nevertheless. Which means that, whereas I don't appear from the diary to have any particularly strong motive for killing him, you two certainly had.

Peter I wouldn't say that at all.

Jane No? Not the discarded mistress and the dismissed faithful employees?

Peter Oh, come off it. We might be upset—angry even—but hardly likely to commit murder.

Jane People have killed for less.

Peter Maybe—but not normal rational people like us.

Jane How do you know that you're normal or rational? Who knows what you might do if you were driven to it?

Peter (*rising*) That's nonsense and you know it.

Jane I don't think that at all. I would say that there was enough evidence to make the police reasonably suspicious.

Peter But this is all hypothetical. We didn't kill him. You did.

Jane I know that and you know it but are the police likely to believe you?

Peter Why shouldn't they believe us?

Jane It's my word against yours, isn't it?

Peter I don't understand. How can it be your word against ours?

Jane Just suppose that I was to tell the police that I saw you kill David.

Peter But you didn't.

Jane I didn't say I did. What I said was supposing I told the police I did.

Peter But you wouldn't. Why should you?

Jane Oh, but I would. Make no mistake about that. If you go to the police and tell them that I've killed David, I'll tell them that I came into this room, during the night, and watched you kill him.

Peter You're bluffing.

Jane Believe me, I'm not. I'll tell them that the three of you—

David and you and Robyn—had too much to drink and that I
went off to bed and left you down here to sleep it off. Then,
later on, I heard raised voices and came down to find out what
was going on. When I came into the room, Robyn was standing
by the settee leaning over David's dead body.

Robyn (*rising*) But how am I supposed to have killed him, for
God's sake?

Jane How do you think? You stabbed him through the heart
with a hat pin of course.

Robyn Me? But I didn't—I didn't. You know I didn't. You did.

Jane That's what you say, isn't it? I'd tell them you killed him.
You had the motive. I didn't. Remember?

Peter That's absurd and you know it is. How do you expect to
prove it?

Jane If you're sensible and don't go to the police, I won't have
to prove it, will I? But I could prove it if I had to—believe me.

Peter How?

Jane Did you have a good look at the hat pin, Robyn?

Robyn No—not really. I just dropped it on the floor.

Jane Exactly. You should have looked at it—you really should.
If you had, you'd have noticed that it was rather an unusual
one. I went to a great deal of trouble to get it. I bought it at
a junk stall. I'm not going to tell you where, of course, but it
was miles away from here. It would be quite impossible to
trace. I took very great care to make sure of that. It has a very
large smooth head.

Robyn Well?

Jane Plenty of room for nice clear fingerprints.

Peter My God, that's why you planted it in Robyn's bag,
knowing she'd find it and handle it.

Jane You are catching on—aren't you?

Peter But you'd already touched it when . . .

Jane When I killed David? That's right. But it didn't take more
than a second or two to wipe it clean before I put it in Robyn's
bag. Earlier on in the evening, I'd pushed it through the
material of her hat out there in the hall to make sure that there
would be some authentic holes to prove where it came from.
I must say it was a bit of a gamble I took that you'd be wearing
a hat as usual. All the same, I think you'll have to agree I
thought of everything, didn't I?

Robyn You're insane. You won't get away with it.

Jane Won't I? You know, I think that, given average luck, I might. I really do. Well, are you two still going to see the police on you way home?

Robyn You bitch! You bloody bitch! (*She rushes across to Jane and attacks her*)

Peter pulls her off

Peter Don't Robyn—don't—it won't do any good.

He sits Robyn down on the settee

Jane Quite right, Peter—quite right. You're showing some sense at last. You always thought I was stupid, didn't you? "Calamity Jane" you used to call me, didn't you? "Everything that stupid woman does goes wrong, doesn't it?" Well, this time, it's gone right, hasn't it? I've turned out to be someone to be reckoned with at last, haven't I?

Peter (*as though to a child*) Look, Jane, you don't know what you're doing. I'm sorry I shouted at you just now. Let's all remain calm and talk it over and see . . .

Jane Stop bloody humouring me. I'm not a child. I know exactly what I'm doing.

Peter All right—you know what you're doing but let's talk about it all the same.

Jane I don't see what else there is to be said.

Peter But there is. At least be practical. What do you intend to do about David's body? You can't just leave him here.

Jane I don't intend to. Today's Sunday. He can stay where he is for the time being and then, tonight, when it's dark, you two are coming back here and you're going to help me move his body to somewhere where it won't be found.

Peter We are going to do nothing of the kind.

Jane Oh, but you are. You have no alternative, have you? I thought I made that quite clear. You'll do as I say.

Peter Supposing we do help you get rid of David's body, where would we put it?

Jane There are some old tin mines about fifty miles from here just past Oakenhurst. They haven't been used for years. They're quite deep. I went there last week and I managed to force a small opening at the top of one of the shafts just large

enough to get a body through. I covered it over with a piece
of wood but I know exactly where it is. I don't think they're
likely to find him down there, do you?

Peter What if we say we won't help you?

Jane That really is up to you. I can't force you. But if you don't
help me, you'll have to stand the risk of Robyn being arrested
for the murder of her ex-lover, won't you?

Robyn (*rising*) We'll have to do it, Peter. Don't you see that?
We have to help her.

Jane Sensible girl. Right—that's it then. You'd better go. I'll
expect you back here at nine o'clock.

Peter But how will you explain David's disappearance?

Jane Just leave all that to me. I'll pack a couple of suitcases with
some of his things and they'll go down the mine shaft with
him. After a day or two, I'll tell anyone who's interested that
he cleared off without saying where he was going. I'll probably
say that it was another one of his women but that this one
must have been more serious than the others. Perhaps that's
why he gave you the brush off, Robyn. Fits rather well,
doesn't it?

Peter There's just one flaw in the story.

Jane Oh, yes—what's that?

Peter If he intended to run off with this ficticious woman, why
would he bother to give us notice?

Jane Good point. In fact, that worried me for some time but, in
the end, the solution fell right into my lap.

Peter What was it?

Jane That entry in the diary—the words he used. He didn't
actually say anything about dismissing you. What he wrote
was "Tell Peter and Robyn there won't be any jobs for them
after next week". Just the way he phrased it—but it all fits in
beautifully, doesn't it? See what I mean?

Peter God, you've had luck on your side, haven't you?

Jane It's not been all luck—far from it. A great deal of planning
has gone into this—a great deal.

Robyn Come on, Peter—let's get out. I've heard as much as I
want to hear. She's evil—that's what she is.

Peter Right—I'm with you.

He takes Robyn's arm and steers her past Jane towards the door

Jane You won't forget you have an appointment here at nine o'clock, will you?

Peter We're not likely to forget, are we?

Jane Well, just make sure you don't. I have that hat pin hidden away just in case.

Robyn Come on, Peter, for God's sake.

Peter (*checking*) Just hold on a minute, Robyn. I've just thought of something important.

Robyn Not now, Peter—let's go, please.

Peter It won't take a minute. There's just one more question I have to ask.

Jane You can ask. I don't promise to answer.

Peter Why bother to get us involved in this? Why didn't you just kill David and not tell us anything about it?

Jane Ah, yes. Now that really is the sixty-four thousand dollar question, isn't it? I'm surprised you didn't ask it before. The answer's very simple really. There were three reasons. The first was a very practical one. I just didn't think I could have managed to get his body out of here on my own. Does that make sense?

Peter What were the other reasons?

Jane The second reason was Robyn.

Robyn Me? Why me?

Jane All the other women he had played about with were little better than tarts but you—you were different. I won't say I was particularly happy about all the others—let's say I tolerated it—but you—he was serious about you—did you know that?

Robyn But he chucked me.

Jane That's right. I made him. (*She sits on the arm of the settee*)

Robyn You made him—how?

Jane That precious diary of his. I opened the drawer of his desk last week—the day he went up to London to that booksellers' meeting. I'd had a duplicate key made—but that's another story. Anyway, I took out his diary and went round to the public library and made photocopies of every page. No-one knew what I was copying because it was one of those coin-in-the-slot machines, you know. When he arrived back that night I told him what I'd done. Then I told him that, unless he gave you up, I'd send the diary to one of the lurid daily papers.

I doubt if they'd have published it but he wasn't prepared to take the risk—and so he agreed.

Robyn Poor David. Oh, God—poor, poor David.

Peter Getting rid of us from the shop—was that part of the bargain too?

Jane No—that was quite genuine. It was entirely his own idea.

Peter But if you planned to kill him, what was the point in going to all that trouble to get him to give up Robyn? And why tell us now?

Jane You don't understand women at all, do you, Peter? I wanted her to know that I'd won him back. The method I used is immaterial.

Peter And the third reason for involving us—what was that?

Jane It seemed a nice touch to bring you in on it as an insurance against the police ever finding his body and thinking it was me who'd killed him. That hat pin—I don't think it's even silver but it's worth a great deal to me now. As long as I have that pin with Robyn's fingerprints on it, I know that you're not likely to say anything about David's sudden disappearance which might result in a lot of embarrassing investigations. (*Rising*) You won't be late tonight, will you? I'd like to be back here afterwards in time for a good night's sleep.

Robyn and Peter stand looking at Jane for a few moments as though mesmerized and then exit

Jane follows them off

Voices are heard off, then the front door slams

Jane enters the room

There is the sound of a car starting and moving away, off

(*Moving to the high-backed settee*) You owe me fifty pounds. You didn't think I could do it, did you?

David (*sitting up*) You shall have it, my dear. You've earned it. I would never have believed that two, grown-up, sensible people could have been taken in by such utter twaddle.

Jane I wouldn't say it was twaddle exactly—a little far-fetched, perhaps.

David It was that all right. Where are they? How did they take it?

Jane They've gone.

David Gone? You didn't let them go without telling them, did you? We agreed not to let them go without telling them the truth, didn't we?

Jane A few more hours won't make any difference.

David But supposing they do something foolish—like going to the police?

Jane They won't. You heard what they said. They believed every word of it.

David I'm not at all sure we should have done it. I don't think it turned out to be as funny as I thought it would.

Jane Oh, come on, David. It was right up your street—the biggest and most elaborate practical joke you've ever pulled.

David It was your idea in the first place.

Jane I know—but you went along with it, didn't you? Look, if you're worried, I'll give them time to get home and then give them a ring and confess.

David Somehow, I don't think they're going to be very amused.

Jane I think they'll be so relieved they'll forgive us. I really do.

David I wouldn't like to bet on it. (*He gets up from the high-backed settee*) God, I'm stiff. I don't think I shall ever return to any semblance of a normal state again. You want to try lying in one position for all that time without moving. It's purgatory. And do you realize that all the time they were leaning over me, I had to hold my breath—I thought I was going to burst.

Jane Poor David.

David And I got a terrible tickle in my throat at one stage. I thought I would choke. Do you think it's too early for a drink?

Jane Far too early.

David (*moving* C) Yes—I'm sure you're right. Later, perhaps. (*He pauses*) You know, I still can't believe they fell for all that. As if anyone would keep a diary of their sex life and then force their wife to listen while they read it out aloud. I'd say that was stretching credibility to its limits.

Jane Perhaps that's why they believed it—because it was so—well, unusual.

David There were so many things which could have gone wrong. Supposing they'd asked to see the photocopy, for instance.

Jane They didn't though, did they?

David At one time, I thought Peter was going to feel my pulse.

Jane That was a big risk, I admit. I gambled on my shock entrance, when I said I'd killed you, distracting their attention.

David Which, fortunately, it did. I couldn't have held my breath for another second longer. Look, I think I ought to give them a ring and see if they're back yet. They might just go to the police—you never know.

Jane I'm convinced they won't—but even if they do, they're going to feel a bit silly when the police turn up here and find you knocking back a large Scotch, aren't they?

David I hadn't thought of that. You're right, of course. But what if they do take it badly? It wasn't really very funny now that I look at it objectively.

Jane They'll be all right, I tell you.

David I couldn't afford to lose them from the shop. They're indispensable.

Jane As I said before, they may be a bit upset to begin with but they'll see the joke in the end.

David I wish I was so sure.

Jane Don't worry about it so much.

David But what about Robyn? I've treated her rather badly, haven't I?

Jane No worse than you treated all the others.

David But Robyn isn't like all the others—she's something special.

Jane Yes, David, I know. But do remember, it was your idea to throw her over, not mine.

David Did I have any choice? You never seemed to have minded about the others but with her it was different. You never gave me a second's peace.

Jane No.

David (*after a pause*) I wouldn't be at all surprised if they don't talk it over when they get home and realize there are loopholes in the story you could drive the proverbial horse and cart through.

Jane Oh, no, David, as long as they think you're dead they'll go on believing it—utterly.

David Maybe.

Jane I know they will. To begin with, I wasn't certain, of course. If I had really killed you, as I said I had, I'd have been taking an almost impossible risk. There were so many things they could have challenged and, in the end, they might have decided not to go along with my plan—go to the police even. Then I would have had it. I knew, though, that if I could get them to agree to helping me dispose of the body they'd be hooked. They would be far too deeply involved to risk the whole business being investigated.

David You make it sound as though it really happened. I don't see why it matters now whether they believed it or not, or if they were prepared to help get rid of the body.

Jane Oh, but it does. It matters a great deal to me.

David Don't sound so serious about it.

Jane But I am.

David I don't understand. It was all a rather stupid joke.

Jane Was it? I had every motive for killing you, hadn't I? I still have.

David Stop fooling, Jane—it was just a joke, I say.

Jane You may have thought so. I wanted you to think that.

David What do you mean?

Jane I've said a lot of things today which weren't true but there was one thing I told Robyn and Peter which was perfectly true.

David What was that?

Jane When I told them how I felt about you. (*She pauses*) I loathe you, David Valentine. I loathe you—do you understand?

David Jane, please—I've had enough jokes for one day.

Jane This is no joke, believe me.

David Then, what . . .

Jane They swallowed my story and they'll go on believing it to be true. As long as there's a body, they'll have no reason to doubt it, will they? They're coming back here tonight at nine o'clock. They're expecting to have to help me to dispose of a body aren't they?

David Until you tell them the truth—yes, I suppose they are.

Jane And if I don't tell them?

David But you will.

Jane Supposing there is a body after all.

David But there won't be, will there?

Jane takes her handkerchief from her pocket and starts to unfold it

Jane! What are you doing?

She starts to move towards him slowly, the hat pin in her hand

Jane, what are you doing with that hat pin? Jane?

Jane moves towards David, who stands as if paralysed, as the Lights slowly fade and—

the CURTAIN *falls*

FURNITURE AND PROPERTY LIST

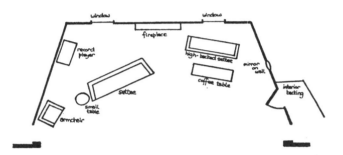

On stage: High-backed settee (facing window)
Coffee table. *On it:* bottles of drink, glasses, **Robyn's** hand-
bag containing comb, lipstick, tissues, hat pin
Settee
Small table. *On it:* dirty glasses
Armchair
Record player. *On turntable:* record
Fireplace. *Above it:* mantleshelf
Window curtains
Carpet
On wall up stage from door: mirror
On floor C: full ashtray

Off stage: Tray with coffee-pot, three cups and saucers (**Jane**)

Personal: **Peter:** watch
Jane: watch
Jane: handkerchief

LIGHTING PLOT

Property fittings required: nil

Interior. A living-room

To open: Dim overall lighting

Cue 1   **Peter** opens R window curtains   (Page 1)
          Increase lighting to give daylight effect

Cue 2   **Peter** opens L window curtains   (Page 2)
          Increase daylight effect

Cue 3   **David:** ". . . with that hat pin? Jane?"   (Page 24)
          Slow fade as CURTAIN *falls*

EFFECTS PLOT

Cue 1   As CURTAIN rises   (Page 1)
            Run-out of record repeating over and over again

Cue 2   **Peter** turns off record player   (Page 1)
            Run-out of record stops

Cue 3   **Robyn** and **Peter** exit, followed by **Jane**   (Page 20)
            Pause, then door slams

Cue 4   **Jane** comes back into room   (Page 20)
            Car starts and moves off

.

Lightning Source UK Ltd.
Milton Keynes UK
UKOW06f1434070915

258217UK00001B/21/P

A MEMC

HIS

BRAVE

HEART

My Husband's Journey

from LVAD to Heart Transplant

R.H.W. DORSEY

Second Acts Press

Cover graphics produced on www.canva.com
Cover photo by R.H.W. Dorsey

Printed in the United States of America

First paperback edition January 2020

ISBN: 978-1-7332702-4-3

Second Acts Press

www.secondactspress.com

Dedication

To Rick, the husband of my dreams. Your unconditional love warms my heart every day and has never failed for a second. You, my love, were worth the wait.

US

Time is catching up to us
I realized the other day
while watching us move about
a house that has existed
lifetimes without you and I
finding each other at last

and thankfully not too late.
Oh, the thought of cheating time
that would not last for too long
though I sometimes wish we could.
We agreed to be grateful
for borrowed time and future

days of blessings yet to come.
You and I laugh together
and try not to sweat the small stuff
of illnesses and ailments
that should bring deep depression
but we grew stronger in bond

and stood in the face of
our obstacles dauntlessly
accepting luck that began
with us finding each other.
We now concede there's no luck
as our story proves it so.

Our union was set in time
and the gift that God's grace has
given us will be our guide.

©2016 R.H.W. Dorsey

Table of Contents

ACKNOWLEDGMENTS

Our journey from my husband's heart failure to his heart transplant involved many dedicated medical professionals, family members, and friends. Skilled surgeons and medical professionals at all levels were instrumental in Rick's medical success story up to the present time. To date, we can't thank the medical staff involved throughout the years enough for their dedication and care. The support received by family members and friends made a huge difference in our emotional strength during the entire heart failure crisis.

Words to thank the heart donor's family aren't adequate for the gift of additional years afforded to Rick. We pray the memory of the donor's sacrifice and its benefits offer some solace to a family who lost one of their own.

We give honor to God for Rick's continued health, our life together and the future ahead.

INTRODUCTION

I've wanted to write this book for a while. In 2017, my husband Rick received a new heart. We experienced a whirlwind and sometimes harrowing ride leading to his life-saving heart transplant. As his wife and caregiver over these years, I can say *we* experienced the journey. However, I take no credit for the absolute bravery and strength in mind and body of my husband. My hope in writing about our experiences is to encourage others finding themselves in our situation. The diagnosis of heart failure was intimidating. Here's where the saying "*God doesn't give you more than you can handle*" comes to my mind. I'm here to tell you the phrase has merit and it remains true for me and my husband to this day. The diagnosis of heart failure immediately caused us to wonder about our future. My husband's heart issues got progressively worse after our second and third year together. The realization our future together may be cut short was an emotional blow. Uncertainty in the future is a fact with heart failure. The only thing Rick and I knew with certainty, in the beginning, was we'd face whatever came our way together.

This book follows our life during the period of my husband's heart failure treatment; Left Ventricular Assist Device (LVAD) placement; and, to him being the recipient of a donor's heart.

PROLOGUE

The temperature was in the mid-fifties on an early Spring day in 2004. I was fearless standing at the downtown train station in my southwestern Pennsylvania hometown. We'd both anticipated this day for many months. Our plans for after his arrival in my city were set. Dinner reservations, tickets to a stage play, and plans to meet some of my family were on our agenda. I'd arrived at the train station early enough to fuss with my hair and makeup in the women's restroom even more than I did before I'd left home. I sat in the lower lobby of the station waiting for who I knew was the man of my dreams. When the arrival of his train was announced, I thought I'd surely have enough time to get one last look in the restroom's mirror. Many months of phone calls and emails brought us to our first face-to-face meeting. We didn't feel like strangers, and we'd already come to an understanding we had something special. As I left the restroom and walked back into the station's lobby, I saw Rick standing at the bottom of the escalator. He wore a leather bomber type jacket and faded blue jeans. He looked lost as I watched him turn his head to scan the train station lobby. I started to yell to get his attention, but I walked toward him instead. When Rick finally caught my eye, he smiled and ran toward me. "Hi beautiful," were his first words to me as he leaned in for our first kiss. My feet weren't planted firmly because when he ran up to me, I stumbled and almost fell backward. Thankfully, Rick caught me as I got my bearings. This is a true story, by the way.

As Rick loaded his luggage in my car, a group of women who appeared to be of senior age walked out of the train station. One of the women yelled across the parking lot, "Well?" She and the other women looked in our direction.

I looked at Rick and wondered if he knew why the women were looking at us. He smiled and said, "They were on my train. I told them I was going to ask you to marry me when I saw you."

"Well?" I said wearing a grin on my face.

"Will you marry me?" He asked as he bent on one knee.

"Yes."

"She said yes!" Rick yelled and looked in the direction of the women standing across the parking lot. We watched as the women clapped and cheered. To me, it was kismet.

Later in the year, we married and began our life together. I remember telling Rick someday I'd write a book about us. Of course, this book isn't the story I thought I'd write. Life has taught me to expect the unexpected. It's our story and we're blessed to share our journey.

"Walk with me into our future dauntless as we journey together in love."

©2012 R.H.W. Dorsey

CHAPTER 1: Transitions

We married seven months after Rick stepped off the train on the Spring day in 2004 (*see Prologue*). The honeymoon stage of our marriage was still in full force through the year 2005. Rick and I took weekend trips, spent Sundays together at our church, and spent time with my local family.

My mother was a genuine person with no problem verbalizing how she felt. She couldn't say enough good things about Rick. My husband was by my side for every single visit with my mother during her illness. As our family said goodbye to my mother at her hospital bedside, Rick was a pillar of strength for us all during her transition from this life. To me, it was a blessing my mother had gotten to know and love Rick before her passing. Although I didn't know Rick's family before we were married, he spoke with love about them. Since he'd always spoken so well about his late mother and father, I knew from the beginning he'd treat my own well.

My father was pleasantly surprised when Rick visited him and asked for my hand in marriage. As a previously married woman in my forties at the time, I loved Rick even more for giving my father the respect of asking. My father loved and respected Rick.

In 2006, Rick had a hospital admission for a mild heart attack. It was recommended he stop smoking to avoid further damage to his heart, lungs, and body. We went about our lives happy and trying to maintain our health.

By the time 2007 came around, we were still enjoying our life together which felt like an extended honeymoon mode. I was working in an underwriting department of an insurance company. Rick was hired by an agency to work in corporate security shortly after we married. Initially, he worked in varying locations around the city. The agency was very impressed with Rick's prior military service and experience. His employer acknowledged he was over-qualified for the duties of the position he accepted. However, my husband was happy for the opportunity and the work. Rick was eventually placed by his agency in the adjoining building of where my company's corporate headquarters and offices were located. We couldn't have been happier commuting to and from work together.

During the time, we took many overnight weekend trips to relax. Our destinations weren't too far from home. Approximately eighteen months into our marriage, we relocated from the city to a suburb outside of town. Rick joined the neighborhood VFW in our new area and settled in well. At work, my husband became well known throughout both office buildings. It wasn't uncommon for someone I didn't know to ask me if I was Rick's wife. We'd have lunch together whenever our schedules permitted. I remember Rick being granted time off from work on a Veteran's Day to participate in a downtown parade with his VFW post. Even though I had to work, I made sure to schedule a time to leave the office to see my husband in the parade. I remember beaming with pride as I watched my husband with the many military veterans being honored.

Rick's time in the military jumping from planes was the primary reason for his deteriorating knees. Pain and swelling had become a fact of Rick's daily life. His old saying "I'll eat the pain" was wearing thin along with his bad knee. After a while, his daily duties of walking around the buildings and stair climbing were becoming more difficult with the increased pain in his knee. It became time for Rick to concentrate on physical therapy, treatments for his knee pain, and lifestyle changes.

By mid-summer in 2007, it was apparent he had to leave his job. Rick got a very nice send-off by his coworkers, building employees, and acquaintances. There were lots of greeting cards and gifts given to him on his last day at work. Rick looked forward to what was to come next.

After the therapies and knee treatments stabilized his knee condition, Rick made the decision to pursue something he'd wanted for a long time. He planned to get a four-year college degree. His interest was in American history. Rick hoped to possibly teach the subject of history one day. Because of his prior military service, he qualified for educational assistance. He was required to enroll in a program of study close to his military experience. After meeting with a representative at the Veterans Administration, Rick found out a teaching course of study wouldn't be approved. He ended up enrolling in a Criminal Justice program at a local university.

Rick enjoyed getting to know some of his younger classmates. In one of his college classes, Rick met the son of a man he'd played against when he was a high school football athlete. I remember joking with my husband and asking him if he was feeling his age. Rick got to know a handful of the university's sports athletes. A few of those younger classmates went on to have careers in professional sports. As much as Rick enjoyed commuting and experiencing life as an older student, there was an adjustment period. Some of the more technical educational tools and electronic software were a challenge. Rick had a basic knowledge of computers. Before enrolling at the university, he was proud of the fact he didn't use a computer unless there was an absolute need. He had to realize quickly he'd be using the same new technology he resisted in his new college classes.

Rick found his life experience and willingness to learn proved useful at the university. He especially enjoyed class discussions where latter twentieth-century historical content was involved. In his history courses, Rick realized immediately by the makeup of students, the majority were too young to remember some of the world events he'd lived through which were up for discussion. He told me how his comments and insights on his life experiences seemed to be appreciated by the instructors as well as the younger college students.

Outside of his campus life, Rick would sometimes get into long discussions with family and friends about historic events. Rick would end up giving an impromptu history lesson during some of those long discussions. I'm still amazed at how my husband retains most of what he learned in high school. He sometimes puts me to shame when we watch the television game show Jeopardy with his broad knowledge.

Rick was excited about most of the coursework. I say *most* because there were a few courses worth cringing. There's not much I've seen to make my husband cringe. I remember one of his required classes which fell in the cringe-worthy category. The name of the course implied a survey of music from the past fifty years. Based on the available course selections at the time, Rick thought the elective course would be a pleasant experience. He also needed a class to fulfill a degree requirement.

After enrolling in the music course and reading the syllabus, Rick found out the course wasn't what he expected. The actual coursework involved the framework of classical music in the twentieth century as applied to modernism and postmodernism. Class exercises included listening to audio files of classical music selections and completing reports on each musical piece. Essays from selected composers were required readings for class discussions. Rick had less than zero percent interest in the class after reading the syllabus. As a music lover myself, I tried my best to be enthusiastic as I read the syllabus. Rick and I ended up laughing out loud about how he was going to get through the course. Dropping the course wasn't an option due to the lack of other selections fitting his schedule. Expressing thoughts, feelings, symbolism, and tone of music in those weekly reports was mentally grueling for him. He'd always avoided subjects involving what he called 'touchy-feely' stuff. The music course would've been a challenge for even me - a lover of most *touchy-feely* things. In the end, Rick got through the course with a passing grade. He vowed never to take a music theory class again. I don't blame him one bit. No offense to any of you music theorists out there. The course wasn't either of our cups of tea.

Rick was quick to learn what he needed to navigate being a middle-aged college student. I believe his one-on-one communication skills played a large part in his enjoyment of working toward a degree. He absolutely loved being a student again.

Unfortunately, the physical issues concerning his knees got worse over time. Rick had to put an end to his degree studies and again concentrate on his health. During that time, I continued to work. We were blessed with grandchildren – one local, and one living in another state. We felt as if we were living the dream.

By early 2009, Rick's knee continued to deteriorate. Months of hospital emergency room visits and follow-up care became part of his normal routine. Chronic knee swelling and pain resulted in multiple medical visits for Rick. Traveling by car to the emergency room was tricky. I didn't have the physical strength to have him bear most of his weight on me to get from our door to the car. He couldn't bear weight on his knee when the accumulated fluid caused swelling and pain. Rick had to literally hop on one foot and lean on me as we made our way from the house to the car at the end of the walkway. We didn't have a wheelchair or crutches available at home during those initial emergency room visits for his knee issues. I remember pulling the car into the ambulance entrance of the hospital on several of those emergency department visits. Showing up without an ambulance at that entrance was frowned on by the staff, but we weren't turned away. The regular emergency room entrance of our local Veteran's hospital was located on a side of the building which was opposite the parking garage. The parking garage was the only place to park at the hospital unless one wanted a long walk from a nearby residential street. Obviously, walking blocks to the hospital wasn't an option at the time. After arriving in the parking garage on some of the emergency room visits, we'd have to hope a spare wheelchair would be available near the elevators on our parking level. Otherwise, Rick had to hop on one foot from the car to the elevator. After arriving on the main floor, we had to walk a good distance to the main lobby area to retrieve a spare wheelchair. Then, it was off to the emergency department further down the hallway. You might question why I didn't take the elevator to the main floor and find a wheelchair in the lobby. My answer would be I tried but my husband wasn't having any of it.

Rick had steroid injections and multiple knee draining done in the emergency department over a long period of time. Prior diagnostic tests and x-rays confirmed total knee replacement was needed. Both knees had issues, but one knee was much worse. The knee surgery was finally performed in the Spring of 2009. The surgery wasn't a complete success. Rick had range-of-motion and extension issues in his replaced knee. After hospital discharge, Rick was transferred directly to the local Veteran's rehabilitation hospital. He recuperated and received aggressive physical therapy for approximately four weeks. I was able to visit him after my workday and spend time with him on the weekends. He was as eager to come back home as I was to welcome him.

At the time, I started to experience physical issues of my own. In the summer of 2009, I began having acute respiratory issues. I had to take time from work for a while. By late summer, pulmonary issues led to my first inpatient hospitalization in close to thirty years. My primary doctor at the time heard my voice over the phone when I called for medical advice. My doctor asked to speak to Rick and told him a trip to the hospital should be made immediately. Rick rushed me to the hospital where I received emergency care. I was evaluated and diagnosed with pneumonia. My chronic asthma didn't make the condition any easier to treat. I was usually the one in the family who took care of everyone else. Being hospitalized and needy was a new reality for me. I recuperated at home after a time in the hospital. While it took some time, I was fortunate to bounce back and return to work after a while. Rick was a godsend whenever I was down and out. Whenever I'd thank him for anything, he'd always say, "That's what I'm supposed to do." As a spouse, I'd expect no less, but it's a great feeling to know you have someone to go the distance with you through life.

CHAPTER 2: Facing CHF

Rick spent lots of time at the VFW and eventually became an officer. He'd had some heart issues in the past, but nothing as serious as the level of congestive heart failure his doctors spoke with us about. My memory is vivid of the day we got the results of the heart catheterization and a few other diagnostic tests for Rick. My years of working with medical claims review at a health insurance company made me familiar with most of the medical terminology the cardiac team used in their explanation of his condition. However, I don't think my brain processed the information the moment it was explained. We were told Rick's heart was failing and he'd eventually need a new heart to survive. At this moment in time, Rick was confined to the hospital due to issues he had with shortness of breath. We sat in his hospital room and received the news together. The medical staff explained Rick had a low ejection fraction. Their explanation of the term was his heart wasn't pumping enough blood to his body.

Later the same day after I'd left the hospital, I remember pumping gas at the Sheetz convenience store in my neighborhood. I received a call from my daughter as I stood by the side of my car with the gas pump in my hand. I answered my cellphone and informed my daughter Rick needed a heart transplant. At the exact moment I spoke the words out loud, I burst into tears. I needed the cry as much as I needed the silent pity party later the same evening at home.

Our VFW was very helpful during the time of Rick's heart failure diagnosis. We began to hope and pray Rick would be considered for a heart transplant. Over time we learned there were many hurdles and health issues to consider before a heart transplant would be a realistic outcome for my husband.

During this time, Rick and I were caring for an aunt who was in her late seventies with health issues. She had a health scare a couple of years after Rick and I were married, so we moved her into our home. My aunt played a huge part in my upbringing. With no children of her own, my aunt has been a second mother to me over the years. Rick treats my aunt like a son would a loving mother and he spoils us both.

It was near the end of 2009 when my medical issues came to a head and I had to stop working. The months of physical therapy and pain were rough for me. My medical issues directly interfered with being able to perform my duties at work. I decided to resign from my job for medical reasons before any personnel issues arose. I wanted to be able to return to work at some point in the future. I knew we'd take a financial hit but even performing light office duties became difficult. Rick was still well enough to pick up the physical slack of keeping the home during the time.

My husband became my caregiver for a while. I'd think the mutual caregiver experience isn't something many would hope to experience. Caregiving is usually a one-sided experience from what I've seen over the years. I would've been content never being on the patient side of caregiving. I'm grateful to have a husband who walks the walk, as it's said. Our experiences to that point in time made me realize what I knew in my heart to be true: Rick took those *in sickness and in health* vows to heart just as I did.

The diagnosis of heart failure for Rick was still on our minds and we continued with dietary and lifestyle changes. Many things needed to happen before he would be considered a good candidate for a donor's heart. For one, Rick had been a smoker for years and now the medical advice for his condition was to quit smoking. His directions were clear -his smoking needed to stop immediately for any consideration of a heart transplant.

I've been around smokers all my life but was never a smoker. As a teen, I bought a pack of cigarettes and hid them in a coat pocket in my bedroom closet. I coughed profusely and felt sick after trying my first cigarette all those years ago. From then on, I knew cigarette smoking wasn't a thing I'd try again. I witnessed my mother quit smoking *cold turkey* when I was growing up.

At the time, Rick had a hard time quitting smoking like many other people with the habit. The doctor prescribed a drug to help him quit smoking. He tried the patch form of the medicine but had terrible side effects. We weren't sure if his side effects were the new drug or a result of its combination with his current medications.

My journal entries from the Spring of 2010 detailed the fears I had about Rick not being able to quit smoking. I wrote in my journal about how devastated I'd be if I lost him only a handful of years after finding him – the man I'd waited for my entire life. During the time when Rick was trying to quit smoking, I'd smell smoke on his clothes when he'd come into the house. I never saw him smoking. Rick was respectful of my allergies to smoke. Nonetheless, seeing or not seeing him smoke was far from the issue. It wasn't lost on me a habit like smoking was hard to quit for some. Rick assured me he was trying to quit smoking and was cutting down. The physicians and a cardiac nurse made it clear in no uncertain terms the smoking must stop. Consideration for a future heart transplant depended on Rick's cooperation in the medical treatment plan. There were blood labs taken at his medical appointments as well as the emergency room visits. My husband admitted he was still smoking. The lab test results confirmed to his medical team smoking was still an issue. One of my sisters, a long-time smoker told me at the time I should understand smoking is a hard habit to kick. I believed what she said to be true. I was never a smoker and couldn't relate to whatever physical or mental issues were involved with trying to quit smoking.

I'd like to think the turning point on his bout with smoking came during the time we had many long discussions about our future.

We would talk about plans for our retirement and living longer to see the grandchildren get older. I remember getting upset once when Rick and I talked about his smoking. The fear of losing him was weighing on me as it would for anyone watching their spouse get sicker over time. I asked my husband what's the point of wanting a long life together if his continued smoking was going to make sure his life was cut short? I was terrified of losing him and wanted him to have a fighting chance to survive. I remember clearly how Rick looked me in the eyes and said, "I'm not giving up on us." I believe the reality of our situation kicked in for both of us at that moment. Rick assured me he was looking forward to our future together as much as I. More grandchildren were on the way on both sides of our family and we saw it as a blessing. Soon after the conversation, my husband stopped smoking with no help from medications. He did it cold turkey.

The year 2010 was transitional for me, also. My health issues and career were priorities needing special handling. I wanted to go back to work as soon as my body would cooperate in the process. As I got stronger, I began making plans to go back to work.

Rick re-enrolled at the university and continued his studies toward his degree. I'd already returned to work by early 2011, but at a different job and a new career. I had years of service and a retirement package with my previous employer. Rick continued to have heart failure issues but maintained his studies at the university for as long as he could. Shortness of breath and fatigue became common for Rick when his body retained more fluid. Medications to reduce the fluid were prescribed. Changes to his diet were ordered including careful monitoring of the sodium intake. When his congestive heart failure symptoms continued to interfere with his normal activities, Rick had to stop his degree studies once again.

Since he was no longer commuting to the university, Rick tried to maintain as active a lifestyle at home as possible. He maintained the household and assisted my aunt with her meals during the day, as well as doing laundry and chores. I'm still amazed when I think of all he did physically with his failing heart. I'm sure Rick handled all the chores and duties slower than before the illness, but he handled them. We both agreed years later those daily activities during the time helped him stay fit and healthy enough to sustain his life even with his heart failure condition.

CHAPTER 3: Digging in our heels

By early 2012, Rick was having increased issues with his heart failure. He seemed to have what we learned were the typical symptoms of heart failure: the increased water retention, swollen legs, constant cough, and shortness of breath. There were times when Rick couldn't lay flat on the bed. He'd prop himself up in bed to help breathe better. At other times, he'd try to rest upright in the easy chair. Considering Rick's previously active life in the military, he became frustrated about his quality of life, and rightly so. He'd been trained to get up early and keep moving.

His long years of military service required him to stay in shape. I was blessed to experience Rick never letting his frustration affect our relationship. Rick has a strength of spirit I'd never seen up close before. His respect and care toward me no matter how he's physically feeling continues to be a beautiful thing.

With the spring of 2012 came multiple VFW duties he needed to power through. Spring at the VFW was busy. Multiple events are held in the Spring including VFW Buddy Poppy drives which benefit veterans' programs at the state and national level. The annual placing of the wreaths on veterans' graves that Spring was a physical challenge for him. This pre-Memorial Day event of placing American flags at gravesites was normally held by his VFW post a week or more before the holiday. The walking and bending in the warm weather at the cemeteries proved to be a lot for Rick. During his duties, Rick had shortness of breath episodes, but he did what he could. It took a couple of his VFW comrades to make him quit for the day. The next week he marched and called cadence with his VFW unit in a neighborhood Memorial Day parade. Ok, I'll say it already, what a man.

Rick's heart failure worsened in the following months. Luckily, later in the summer of 2012, we were able to take a long-awaited trip back to Rick's hometown where most of his biological family lived. The trip back home was extra important as we knew Rick's condition was getting worse. I knew to see his family back home always gave him a boost in energy. We needed to make the trip happen and did.

Sometime after we returned home from the trip, Rick was hospitalized and admitted to the intensive care unit for heart failure. The oral medications he was taking at the time for his congestive heart failure and blood pressure were no longer as effective since his heart was getting weaker. A drug named Milrinone was given to Rick intravenously in the hospital. We were told the drug would make his heart pump harder by lowering his blood pressure and improving his blood flow. The Milrinone stabilized Rick's condition enough for him to return home. At discharge, he was given a portable infusion device to receive the medication intravenously at home. We were told the intravenous pump wasn't a permanent solution, but it would help Rick's heart which was in the advanced stages of failing.

Lifestyle changes and an even more restricted low sodium and heart-healthy diet were now required for my husband. Visiting nurses came to our home to get blood labs, administer necessary medications, and check the pump was infusing medication correctly. We got instructions on how to use the portable infusion pump including replacing the tubing when necessary. At home as a caregiver for my husband, I was able to help Rick with the blood pressure, temperature and necessary weight checks. Rick and I had to learn about abnormalities and symptoms to look for and when to call for advice or help. The home care companies had staff on standby around the clock for guidance. The intravenous medication pump was helpful, but emergency hospital visits were still a reality.

The emergency room visits became so common during the time, we sometimes anticipated the outcome. The drill became familiar: Rick would experience severe shortness of breath; we'd head to the Veterans hospital emergency department; initial evaluation of Rick was done by the medical staff; diagnostic and blood tests were run; and, intravenous diuretics were administered to him. Depending on his blood pressure status and other medical issues, Rick would either get discharged to home or have an inpatient stay for a day or so. There were times we prepared a *go-bag* for the hospital in advance.

We found out during those times how much he and I had a *do what you need to do attitude*. However, the entire situation wasn't easy for either of us emotionally. There were many times when we felt mentally and physically drained. The middle of the night emergency room visits became the most taxing because of the lack of sleep. The bouts of shortness of breath would often happen to Rick while we both were in a deep sleep. "Honey, we have to go to the hospital", Rick would say in the dark of night. Knowing my husband, I knew he must have needed medical help if he didn't wait until morning. Sometimes, in his stubbornness (*God love him*) my husband would wait until morning to admit he felt the need to go to the hospital. Rick is your average, stubborn, ex-military first sergeant I was told by a person with military experience who knew people like him. Luckily, on all those emergency room visits, we were fortunate to get Rick to the hospital in enough time to get his fluids and blood pressure under control.

Short stays in the hospital were common and frequent for Rick by the time October of 2012 arrived. I was able to retrieve a post on my social media Facebook feed during that time. My post of early October of 2012 reads:

"I'm happy tonight that Rick is back home where he belongs. It'll be a long road, but we're 'digging in our heels' in Rick's words. Thank you, family and friends, that kept him, in your thoughts and prayers and asked about him. We both know we're blessed, and God has this!"

One of the good things I can admit about social media and namely Facebook is the platform served as a great source for my memory banks. I kept personal journals throughout my adult life but not as consistent as I believed I should've done, in retrospect. There are gaps of years between some of my personal journal entries in my files. So, I'm now relying on my social media timelines and iPhone note entries to boost my memory while writing this book.

In between the medical visits and hospital stays, there was still time to enjoy our life. The enjoyment was at a new pace. Rick still had his regular VFW duties. We both participated in our VFW's annual Christmas shopping for toys and wrapping gifts for the children's holiday party that year. I was able to keep up with my VFW Ladies Auxiliary duties as well.

One of my friends wisely told me early in Rick's illness, "Be sure to document your experiences during your happiest and saddest moments." I documented some things, but not as thoroughly and consistently as I'd planned. Personally, when I reflect on our adventures (and we both admit we see our lives together as an adventure), it gives me renewed strength. I'm reminded of how far Rick and I have come on what can be called a medical adventure. The necessity to write a book may not be for everyone in our situation, but the process is cathartic for some, like me.

CHAPTER 4: Hope and the LVAD

Multiple diagnostic tests were taken in the last quarter of 2012 for possible evaluation of the Left Ventricular Assist Device (LVAD) implantation in Rick. He had a good team of physicians at the local Veterans hospital. During the last quarter of the year, I have to say, one physician, who I'll call Dr. J, was a lifesaver for Rick. I recall Rick and I got information about the LVAD and how scary the prospect seemed. We received a small amount of literature about the device termed by some of the medical staff as a mechanical heart pump. The idea of an actual device inside his chest doing most of the work for the heart was intimidating to both of us. We were informed the intravenous medication pump was no longer working effectively to combat Rick's heart failure. The long-term prognosis for my husband's survival with medication only was bleak. We were told by medical staff a donor heart could take years due to Rick's blood type. We came to realize time waiting for a donor's heart wasn't a luxury without some other intervention.

The symptoms of heart failure were getting worse as the weeks passed. The decision to be considered for the LVAD was an easy one. Rick chose to fight and was open to all prospects to make his survival a reality. We discussed everything and weighed limited medical options. We, and more importantly Rick, agreed the LVAD was the option we wanted to take. It sounded great, so sign him up, right? It wasn't so easy by a long shot.

We learned one of the important medical factors was controlling Rick's blood pressure. He had several diagnostic procedures to monitor pulmonary hypertension before December of 2012. A cardiac physician, Dr. J, as I noted earlier, requested a consult with a Veterans Administration hospital out of state that performed LVAD surgeries. Our local Veterans hospital didn't have a transplant or LVAD surgery program at the time. There were a couple of setbacks in Rick's condition. The medical staff informed us that Rick didn't meet the criteria for serious consideration of LVAD implantation. I remember the doctors saying Rick's pulmonary pressures and his kidney function needed to improve. We were discouraged but hopeful and believed God was on our side.

Dr. J didn't give up trying to find hospital programs that accepted higher risk LVAD candidates like Rick. There was a local world-renowned hospital with a heart transplant program. However, Rick's care needed to be done at a Veterans hospital if possible, for both bureaucratic and mainly financial reasons. We held out hope Rick's condition would stabilize to the point of getting a consult with the LVAD team at the Veterans hospital out of state. Sadly, Rick was unable to get on the UNOS (United

Network for Organ Sharing) list at the time. Therefore, the LVAD was what we'd hope would save his life and give him more time for a heart.

Luckily, Rick's lung pressures temporarily stabilized in December of 2012 and we got the green light to visit the out of state hospital for evaluation of an LVAD transplantation. My understanding was Dr. J's diligence made the evaluation possible. The out-of-state Veterans hospital would conduct diagnostic tests and consider if Rick was a candidate for the LVAD. We thanked God for Dr. J, who never gave up on Rick. This is not to say his entire team of physicians, nurses and medical staff weren't attentive or responsive to Rick's care at our local hospital. He was fortunate to have the care and support of the entire cardiac team in our town. We continue to give thanks to all who helped get Rick to the VA Medical Center in Richmond, VA.

Our departure date for Richmond was in the second week of December 2012. I documented on my Facebook social media page:

"Good Monday morning! Flight delayed due to weather but that's ok; just praying for traveling mercies! Have a good day all!"

I didn't remember the flight being delayed since it was so long ago, but again, I'm thankful for my Facebook timeline serving as a memory aid.

Rick was admitted to the VA Medical Center in Richmond for inpatient testing on the day we arrived. I was fortunate to stay in temporary lodging at a hospitality house during this first visit to Richmond. Family members of patients who traveled long distances were referred to receive accommodations at the hospitality house. During my stay, I met many family members of patients confined in the local university and community hospitals. At the time, I was one of the few guests with a family member at the Veterans hospital located across town. The university hospital was located less than a mile away from the hospitality house. A free shuttle traveled from the hospitality house to the university hospital multiple times during the day. The Veterans hospital arranged my travel to their facility across town. A private transportation company was contracted by the Veterans hospital for family members in my situation. I was able to schedule my daily pickup from the hospitality house to the Veterans hospital and my return trip. It was a blessing to support and spend time with Rick as he went through all the required testing.

We met more than a few members of the medical staff during his hospital stay. Rick had to undergo diagnostic testing for a few days as part of the LVAD evaluation. There was also an evaluation of the family support available for Rick should he receive the LVAD. I remember being asked about alternate family member support for my husband. If for any reason I was no longer able to act as a caregiver for Rick, there would need to be an alternate caregiver. A patient's emotional evaluation was also a determining factor in the evaluation process. Of course, there were more detailed medical criteria Rick had to meet before he would be considered.

The stay for the evaluation lasted a few days. We both met with members of the Richmond VA cardiac and LVAD team at the end of the stay in Richmond. We were given the great news Rick would be considered for LVAD implantation. It was encouraging to hear Rick could possibly be called back to Richmond within the next month. The anticipation for January of 2013 was heavy on our minds even before we left for home. Life-saving LVAD surgery was becoming a reality. The unknown was scary, but it didn't change our decision to move forward. The LVAD medical staff made it clear my husband and I had to make the commitment to the surgery. They said the caregiver role in the procedure was key in the recovery process. For me, I needed to know my husband was ready to face the surgery. I prayed about everything and knew whatever my husband's decision was, I would be by his side. I'm glad he chose to move forward. We embraced our faith that God would see us through everything. After the testing was completed, Rick was discharged from the hospital. He joined me at the hospitality house to wait for our flight back home scheduled for the next day.

Unfortunately, a winter storm delayed our flight for a day or two. The day of the rescheduled flight back home was unforgettable. On the morning of December 14, 2012, we completed the final touches of packing luggage in our room at the hospitality house. The television in the room was broadcasting the morning news. The story about the Sandy Hook Elementary School shooting in Newtown, Connecticut was still unfolding. We thought of the victims and the surviving parents and families for a long while after that day. The news reports we watched and read about the Sandy Hook tragedy forced us to put our worries in a proper perspective. At the airport on the day of our return trip home, there was a brief flight delay. My Facebook post from the time reads: *Delayed. Not complaining since it was a promising trip. We'll get there when we get there.*

We arrived back home safely and enjoyed the Christmas holiday with family at a slower pace than normal since Rick still had congestive heart failure issues. There was a lot to be thankful for, no matter what the outcome. Spending time with the family and two of the local grandchildren was the medicine no doctor could prescribe.

The New Year of 2013 was upon us and we anticipated when we would hear from Richmond about scheduling the LVAD surgery. Our local hospital was keeping the Richmond staff informed of Rick's condition during our wait for the LVAD. January of 2013 came and went and there was no word on when we were positively going back to Richmond for the surgery.

By early February 2013, Rick had severe congestive heart failure symptoms. He was hospitalized by mid-February and was in critical condition. The medical crisis was real. Rick needed to get to the Veterans hospital in Richmond for the LVAD surgery as soon as possible. The medical prognosis was if Rick's condition deteriorated further, there was a possibility he'd be too weak to survive the LVAD surgery. I remember there was some type of issue as to when Rick would be transported from the intensive care unit to Richmond. I don't know what the delay was about, but I remember feeling like those were desperate times. Dr. J and others on the cardiac team were concerned about his condition. I remember the look on an ICU nurse's face when I asked how Rick was doing. The nurse would only confirm what the doctors already said, Rick's condition wasn't good. I recall asking family and friends to pray for Rick even more at that time. One of the days during this entire experience that I'll never forget was a day I was talking to Dr. J. The doctor looked at me and said: "I'm going to do whatever I can to get Rick to Richmond fast. He needs to be there now." I believed it and had faith the doctor would try.

The next day, I was home preparing to go to the hospital to visit my husband. I got a call from the hospital transportation services. There was a medical flight to Richmond scheduled for Rick and me in a couple of hours! Fortunately, I didn't have to travel the forty minutes to get to the hospital to leave with Rick. Considering, I was only partially packed I had a short window of time to get everything settled at home. The smaller regional airport where the medical flight would depart was only a few miles away from our home.

I don't know to this day what events occurred to help get Rick approved to go to Richmond during his medical emergency. I'm sure his critical medical status was a huge factor. However, I'm not going to look a gift horse in the mouth as the saying goes. One of our neighbors was home when I got the call. She was able to drive me to the regional airport. We lived in an area where public transportation wasn't within a reasonable walking distance for the average person. A taxicab to the area would take too long as I knew from prior experience. I was grateful to my neighbor for dropping what she was doing to get me to the airport on time. When I got to the airport, the indoor waiting area for the flights had a huge window overlooking the runway. I was told the small plane I saw sitting not far from the building was our transport to Richmond. When I saw how small the plane was, I became anxious. The plane was technically called an air ambulance in our situation. I didn't enjoy flying in general and was always a little nervous on every commercial flight I'd taken in the past. This would be the smallest plane I'd been on to that point, but it didn't matter. Both of us were getting on the plane.

Rick's ambulance transport from the hospital to the small airport ended up getting delayed. When I called the hospital to check why he hadn't arrived, I was told there were medical reasons delaying his departure from the hospital in the city. The air ambulance nurse arrived at the airport before the scheduled take-off time and introduced herself. She told me she takes these flights several times a week, and they're very safe. I remember an airport staff member telling me the plane wasn't going to leave without us since we were the only passengers besides the pilot and nurse. Almost to the minute of the scheduled departure time, the ambulance transporting Rick arrived. I was so happy to see him and noticed how weak he looked. We said a prayer before they wheeled his gurney outside to the waiting plane. My seat on the plane was directly behind the pilot and close enough to have touched his shoulder. The flight nurse attended to Rick while he remained on his back strapped in on a stretcher. In the end, I was pleasantly surprised to have the smoothest plane ride of my life on the air ambulance medical flight. I thanked God for traveling mercies as the plane landed so gracefully on the runway at the Virginia airport.

Rick and I were transported from the Richmond airport by an ambulance which was waiting for our arrival. I rode in the passenger seat of a large ambulance which I believed doubled as a fire truck. Climbing up into the huge truck was interesting and comical, in retrospect. The emergency personnel boosted me up by my backside up into the front passenger seat. I told them to do whatever's needed to get me in the ambulance. The seat bounced up and down during the entire ride. The driver informed me the seats were made with air suspension. We arrived at the hospital emergency room where the waiting medical staff wheeled Rick's gurney to the medical intensive care unit. It took some time to get Rick situated before I could see him again. I was so relieved he'd finally get his fighting chance at a longer life. Knowing the surgery could be performed meant everything to us.

There were medical issues with Rick needing stabilization before he could undergo surgery. When his condition improved, a surgery date was set which was approximately eight days from his original emergency admission date. I stayed at the Fisher House on the hospital property. If you're unfamiliar with Fisher Houses, military and veterans' families are permitted to temporarily live in these homes during the patient's confinement. We were grateful I was able to stay within walking distance of the hospital.

I felt helpless but one thing I could do was ask for prayer requests. I called family and made requests to family and friends online. Even though I was alone in the city with Rick critical in the hospital, I was happy we made it to this turning point of his health crisis. Those first few days of this presurgical confinement were spent anticipating my husband's upcoming LVAD implantation surgery. Any worries about the open-heart surgery were greater than realizing I was alone in an unfamiliar city where I knew no one.

CHAPTER 5: Fighting for Life

We spent our days prior to the LVAD surgery talking to family and friends giving updates on Rick's progress. I brought my iPad with me to take pictures and videos. Rick's body was weakened, but his spirits were high with confidence in the days before the surgery. On one of the days before the surgery, I noticed Rick look at me as I walked into the intensive care room. He was on the bed hooked to multiple monitors. I believe he knew I was fighting tears and trying to put on a brave front for him. He looked at me and said, "Honey, I don't know how to quit." I believed Rick's words. The weeks leading up to this moment was a great example of what my husband said to me. I learned my husband was stronger in spirit than I ever imagined.

Our church family at home was supportive throughout the entire time. While we were away, Rick's name was always on the prayer list. Clergy members at the church would also call to check on Rick's condition. Rick and I both had upbringings in church and knew the faith we had in God was what kept us whole. Our church Pastor in my hometown was the same person who baptized me years before I'd met Rick.

The LVAD surgery was set for the early morning. I was permitted to spend time in Rick's intensive care room most of the day and evening before the surgery. I was told the intensive care unit didn't allow visitors, family members or otherwise, to stay overnight in the patient rooms. The medical staff informed me it was common for family members wanting to stay overnight before major surgery to stay in an area on the same floor. The room wasn't a patient room, but it had a chair that extended to a lounging position. I'd been made aware of the room days before, so I brought an overnight bag the night before his surgery. The room doubled as a vending area but had doors that could be closed. I had to register with the Admissions office to get a tag to stay overnight. I didn't get much sleep at all. I was anxious, nervous, and excited about the surgery.

Rick served in more than a few combat missions in his military career. He'd been lucky and blessed to have survived bullet wounds serving in past active duty. I knew this invasive open-heart surgery would be one of the toughest things he'd have to go through physically. For whatever reason, a few days before, I researched the details of the actual surgical procedure. When I say details, I mean step by step details of the surgery. I was shocked to find a video on an online YouTube channel. The video was of a surgeon performing the LVAD surgery. I decided to watch the video since I'm one of those *need to know* kind of people, most of the time. When I watched the graphic video showing the beating heart being punctured and threaded to attach the LVAD to a heart, I was absolutely frightened for Rick. I wondered how his failing heart could survive that kind of surgery given he'd recently been in extremely critical condition. There was no turning back, though. Besides, my husband wasn't a quitter and I loved he was that type of person. I didn't tell Rick before the surgery I'd watched the video. If you're not a person comfortable with seeing blood, I wouldn't suggest watching a video of the surgery, and especially not the night prior to the surgery.

I was able to see my husband in the early hours on the day of his surgery. He was ready to be prepped and moved to the operating room on another floor. I walked with the staff as they rolled his bed to the surgery area. At the restricted area, the medical attendants stopped rolling the bed so Rick and I could say a few words to each other. Rick grabbed my hand and said, "I'll see you on the other side," with a smile on his face. He'd told me in the past the phrase meant I'll see you when this situation is done. The capacity in which my husband served in the military involved dangerous operations. The scars left on various parts of his body from healed wounds let me know years before this operation Rick was a survivor. He can't and won't talk about a lot of his military experience. I believe his past experiences helped him bravely handle everything this crisis brought. After all, he's one of those heroes who often run toward danger and not away from it.

The cardiac nurse on the team told me the length of the procedure could be longer than seven hours. The LVAD nurse coordinator was a great help in keeping me posted by text message of the progress of the surgery. Knowing everything was going as planned relieved my stress as the surgery progressed. I kept myself busy by sitting in the large open cafeteria area during most of the surgery. The waiting wasn't as bad as I thought it'd be since I had a few video games I enjoyed playing loaded on my iPad. Reading material and calls to friends and family kept me busy for a long while. Sometime in the early evening, the LVAD nurse coordinator sent a text to let me know the surgery was over and Rick pulled through. A short while later, the nurse sent another text indicating Rick was off the bypass machine and the LVAD was pumping for his heart. I felt relief, joy, and thankfulness all at once.

CHAPTER 6: LVAD Recovery & Miracles

In the days following the surgery, Rick had a slow but steady recovery. The breathing tube was to be removed a few days after the surgery. I was slightly worried it would take several days for the tube to be removed. My worries were probably due to having so much information in my head about different phases of the recovery period. I was on information overload. The staff assured me each patient was different, and Rick was progressing well.

The visiting hours in the surgical intensive care unit (SICU) were controlled for patients. Visits were limited to minutes at a time during this critical recovery period. I got to spend more time at the Fisher House meeting some of the residents. I journaled at the time about meeting some of the other houseguests and having breakfast with them in the house a few days after Rick's surgery.

Shortly over a week after the surgery, Rick was still in the SICU. The huge scar left by the open-heart surgery was healing well according to the medical staff. Things were looking up and Rick was at ease. One day that week I sat in the waiting room waiting for the next designated visiting time for Rick. While sitting there, I met the wife of a veteran who was in the SICU. The woman told me her husband had open heart surgery a few months before and he'd fallen into a coma. She told me her husband was recently readmitted and was in critical condition. The woman talked about her discussion with the physicians about the possibility her husband wouldn't recover from the coma. She seemed upset and was worried about never getting to speak with her husband again. She and I talked for a long time as we sat in the SICU waiting area. During that time, one of the SICU nurses who was assigned to both my husband and hers had finished her shift. The nurse walked into the waiting room, looked at both of us and asked, "Can I pray with both of you?" We welcomed the offer and the nurse prayed for both our husbands. I remember this encounter, and these are the additional words I journaled that day:

"One hour later the woman's husband came out of the coma and she was able to talk with him tonight. I'm not surprised because I know it's all in God's hands even when the doctors have given their final word. I was so encouraged to see the power of prayer up close and personal tonight. God is good."

The interaction with the praying nurse was so encouraging not only to that woman but to me as well.

In the next few days after the nurse had prayed for us, Rick's condition took a turn. A week had passed since the surgery. The initial days following the surgery were as expected. There were plans to transfer Rick to the step-down unit for the remainder of his recovery. However, Rick began to experience symptoms warranting a longer stay in the SICU. Some of the normal lab results began to produce abnormal results. The most frightening thing, to me at least, was thinking Rick's congestive heart failure symptoms were returning. The LVAD was supposed to improve the CHF. We knew something was terribly wrong. I learned from the surgeon and medical staff the symptoms Rick was having were a warning the LVAD was not working properly. Of course, the experienced team had a plan to diagnose or confirm what they suspected could be the problem with Rick's now failing health. Additional blood labs, x-rays, and other diagnostic tests were ordered for Rick. I remember feeling so helpless not being able to help my husband in any way.

The result of all the testing was blot clots had formed in his chest on or near the LVAD causing the adverse symptoms. This was a life-threatening outcome that needed a quick solution. We were told that developing blood clots were a risk with LVAD devices. A surgeon on the LVAD team explained to me the clots were causing Rick to have congestive heart failure symptoms which resulted in the abnormal blood lab test results.

I didn't write a lot in my journal at that time, but I remember being in what I sometimes call an *auto-pilot* mode. I promised myself to be strong and if I needed to cry, I'd cry when I wasn't with Rick. Those long bouts of crying were saved for the end of the night before my prayers. The crying was cathartic as I needed to get it out of my system to prepare for the next day. For whatever reason, I felt stronger after a good cry.

When I heard the surgeon say, "we need to open him back up," I had no words. Another open-heart surgery within two weeks of the first was terrifying to me. The surgeon informed Rick and me the subsequent surgery was necessary to remove the clots around the internal LVAD device. The clots were life-threatening. Rick was the consummate trooper. He said to the surgeon, "Let's light this candle." It was the moment I knew my husband was ready for anything. I thought to myself at the time if Rick was scared, he didn't show it. I asked him in later years if he was afraid during that time and his response was "I didn't have time to be scared."

The day of the second surgery and the events are a distant blur in my mind. The post on my social media page to our family and friends during the time reads:

"The doctors said this second surgery went well and Rick is resting tonight. Hopefully, he'll be able to get the breathing tube out tomorrow. Thanks for the prayers. Love you all family and friends!"

What I do remember, however, is a few days following the second surgery. I was at the Fisher House getting ready early in the morning to visit Rick in the surgical intensive care unit. My routine during this time was to call the unit early in the morning to speak with the nurse assigned to Rick for details of how he did overnight. Before I got the chance to call the unit, the nurse gave me a call. She said something to the effect of, "Don't be alarmed, he's ok, but he pulled out his breathing tube. We were going to remove it this morning, but he pulled it out." I rushed to get ready and went to the hospital. I found out later from Rick that he'd heard the staff talking about removing the tube. He said he was groggy, and thought he'd heard someone say to him, "This tube has to come out." Rick explained to me when he was in special operations in the military, he was taught to help the medics. So, after gagging for a bit, he took the tube out. The outcome could have been worse with a stunt like that, but he didn't hurt anything. I couldn't do anything except shake my head in relief at my husband.

Rick spent less than a week in the SICU and was transferred to the step-down unit to finally begin his recovery. We realized how fortunate we were to have the skilled medical team guide his care during that crisis. Only a month before, Rick's survival was uncertain. Now, he had a fighting chance.

CHAPTER 7: The Fisher House

I'd be remiss if I didn't share how the Fisher House was a godsend for Rick and myself on our stay for his LVAD surgery. The Fisher House I stayed in had about twenty or so rooms for families of veterans who were hospitalized at the Richmond Medical Center.

When I arrived the first day after the air ambulance flight in February of 2013, I was met by one of the staff members of the Fisher House. I was given a tour of the house and the house rules and everything I needed to know as a guest was explained to me. The house had a huge kitchen area where house guests could cook meals. There was a long island in the kitchen to accommodate the guests to prepare food, separate pantry space for each guest's personal food items, and a breakfast nook area with a couple of chairs. The large restaurant-sized refrigerators and freezer held donated food as well as designated space for each guest's personal food items. There were also donated pantry items and non-perishables available for guest consumption. The house had a living room area with a large screen TV, sofa, and chairs. A laundry room equipped with washers and dryers was also available for use. The dining room was immaculately designed with beautiful artwork, tables, and chairs. A beautifully landscaped backyard had trees and a lovely gazebo furnished with cushioned patio chairs. The guest bedrooms were spacious with a large closet, small and large dresser with drawers, lamps, and a huge bathroom with a shower and lots of counter space near the sink.

I wanted to give the details of the house because it was such a blessing to walk into that house and not have a worry about my safety, accommodations, or any of the worries one would have traveling away from home. It didn't hurt that the house was like staying in a luxury hotel or someone's beautiful home. The Fisher house was truly my home away from home.

When Rick was finally well enough to be transferred to the step-down unit, I was relieved. I'd become acquainted in those first weeks with a few women guests of the house who were wives, mothers or family members of veterans in the hospital. We all shared stories of how our loved one came to be an inpatient in the hospital. The stories were heartbreaking, miraculous and hopeful. The day following Rick's first day in the step-down unit at the hospital, the group of ladies and I planned our stress-relieving trip out to a local restaurant. Most of our days waiting for our veterans to recuperate were long, emotional and tiring. Some of the veterans were in the fight of their lives, and some were on the road to recovery. We bonded in our similarities of purpose, no matter how different our backgrounds. The veteran in the hospital was the priority and our reason for being there. I believe we all realized sometimes we needed to let our hair down, relax and have fun. We were all experiencing stress at different levels. Taking care of one's self is a hard lesson for a caregiver to learn or master.

Here's the journal entry which I shared on my social media page detailing one of the days around that time:

"Yesterday was a good day. My husband transferred out of the intensive care to a step-down unit, and I had a nice relaxing dinner out with three of the ladies here. We brought our desserts back to the house and stayed up past midnight talking, laughing and asking iPhone Siri stupid questions… just a silly and nice time we all needed for a change."

That day was a good day and I remember it well. I could exhale for the first time in a while with the knowledge Rick was on the road to recovery.

Rick was in the step-down unit in good spirits. He and I tried to normalize things as much as possible as he got over the hurdle of the second open-heart surgery. Like every year, I was able to print out the NCAA March Madness basketball bracket with our picks. I journaled about my busted bracket after the first round. Rick always did better on the brackets since he was a true fan of the sport at the college level.

Houseguests were good about helping other guests and offering rides for fellow guests. Some people in the house needed to venture off the VA property to get groceries or go shopping.

After some time, I realized I needed to rent a car. I was always independent and wanted to be able to get around town at my convenience. When I rented the car, I was able to offer rides to a guest needing to venture off the hospital campus for shopping. Thankfully, there was no charge to stay at the Fisher House so any other expenses during that time were kept to a minimum. One thing I noticed right away was the positive atmosphere of the house. It seemed shared experiences between the houseguests brought out the best in people, including myself. It wasn't uncommon for a new guest to walk into a common area in the house and be greeted by a few of the guests and made welcome. I was able to witness the absolute kindness and helpfulness of complete strangers helping others many times at the Fisher House. I believe people in crisis near others immediately form a common bond of sorts. Caregivers like myself at the Fisher House were in crisis, but in a different way than our family members confined in the hospital.

I saw many guests come and go from the Fisher House while staying there. Most of the houseguests I met were there about a week, or sometimes less. I met people from neighboring states who came for a short stay while their veteran family member recovered in the hospital. There were other guests who alternated time at the house with other caregiver family members. A few of the guests stayed at the house for a couple of months while their veterans were in the hospital.

Shortly after Easter, in April of 2013, Rick was able to discharge to the Fisher House to get outpatient treatment before going home. The LVAD was working great and he recovered well in those weeks following the second surgery.

A highlight of the time in the Fisher House now that Rick was better, was a visit from family. Rick's first cousin and her husband and now my extended family, came from a neighboring state to spend the day with Rick and me at the Fisher House. We were thankful for the visit which was such a boost in Rick's spirits and mine. The last weeks at the Fisher house were spent going to the hospital for outpatient testing and attending some of the veteran-related activities at the hospital. I recall a vintage car show held on the property of the hospital during the Spring. Rick and I enjoyed meeting the veterans along with their friends and family.

Shortly before we were to travel back home, Rick was well enough to ride with me to return the rental car. On our way through the downtown area, I made a wrong turn down a one-way street. I was still unfamiliar with the downtown area streets since I'd mostly ventured in the outskirts of the city. Three lanes of cars were headed straight toward us. Quick thinking, maneuvering, and God's grace saved us that day.

CHAPTER 8: LVAD Education

During Rick's recuperation, he had physical therapy that included timed walks inside the hospital's walking routes. There was constant testing being done to check for any sign of infection. Patient and caregiver instruction on the LVAD and its equipment was required before Rick's discharge. A small device called a controller was worn in a harness outside his body. The controller device had electronic displays indicating how the LVAD was working. Rick and I were instructed on normal and abnormal display values. The batteries for the LVAD powered the device and the controller and were attached to the controller unit. There were multiple rechargeable batteries supplied along with a charging unit. Batteries were constantly charging, and a portable case for the backup batteries and an extra controller was always in the case. If a battery was close to losing power, an alarm would sound on the controller. The controller alarms were always *alarming* to us *(see what I did there?)* because this device was pumping his failing heart that previously threatened to take his life. So, yes, any alarm which sounded got our complete attention. There was a list of alarm types we had to study. We both admitted to each other we felt like we were on information overload. We knew we'd have to keep a cheat sheet for the alarm types handy.

Rick had an opening in his stomach where a driveline tube exited from the device inside his body to the controller unit. The *hole* as some called it needed frequent dressing changes. I had to learn the proper procedures to sterilely change the dressing.

One of the surprising things we learned about the LVAD was that Rick wouldn't have a detectable pulse reading. Rick thought this was a cool thing. When he'd meet someone new, he enjoyed saying, "Feel my wrist, see no pulse!" He'd explain to people that his device was pumping for him. One of the other important patient care routines was to check the blood pressure. I'll leave the technical explanations to the experts on why the normal blood pressure readings wouldn't be accurate on an LVAD patient. What I will say is we had a blood pressure cuff we used to calculate a *mean arterial pressure* (MAP). The MAP had to be within a certain range to show Rick's fluids were within the desired range and the device was functioning as expected. Loving math as I do, I enjoyed calculating the MAP in my head once I had the reading.

We were told to inform our local power company and emergency medical services of Rick's medical condition when we arrived home. There was a letter provided by the medical staff explaining Rick had this life-saving device. In case of a home emergency, such as a power outage or if emergency transport

was required, those entities would know of his condition.

CHAPTER 9: Home, Sweet Home

Finally, it was time to head home. Rick received various gifts and complimentary items from veteran events at the hospital during his stay. I had personal items purchased over time which needed to be shipped home as well. Members of the LVAD team were great in helping both of us expedite our items home. Strangely enough, we still had more than a few luggage items to check and carry on the plane. The initial trip home after the surgery on a commercial flight this time was a new and interesting adventure.

Transporting medical items unfamiliar to the average airport employee proved to be unnerving on the trip home in the Spring of 2013. There was a disagreement at the security check with TSA staff as to whether Rick s should go through the imaging machine with his batteries. One airport staff person almost demanded that Rick remove his batteries. We had to explain again the controller device and batteries were unable to be removed. Apparently, the information on the letter we gave to the first staff member standing a few feet away was not communicated to the other worker. The debacle was not necessary since Rick has shrapnel from previous military injuries that prevented him from going through those machines in the first place. The information about Rick's shrapnel was previously communicated to the TSA staff.

After the security check process, we arrived at the gate and found the flight was delayed. Despite the previous issue at the security check, we had to put everything in perspective. We were going home and feeling so blessed for this day. My online journal for the day we got home read:

"15 hours later now in our living room ...ready to fall into bed ...unpacking will have to wait until later today! Thank you, God, for the traveling mercies!"

In less than a month from the time we arrived home, Rick was back performing duties at our VFW Post. I resumed my Ladies Auxiliary duties, also. My husband's birthday that Spring was extra special, and we spent the day enjoying local attractions he's never seen. We felt procrastination in our lives was no longer feasible. The dressing changes, blood pressure checks, and controller checks were getting easier as the weeks progressed.

One of the many medications Rick was prescribed was to prevent clotting. Bleeding and clotting were among the risks we had to watch for with Rick's LVAD now in place. We made frequent visits to our local Veterans hospital for Rick's outpatient anticoagulation management.

The following month at home we received two bits of sad news about people we'd met at the Medical Center in Richmond. Two of the women I met at the Fisher House lost the family member that was being treated in the hospital. We saw lots of uplifting things at the hospital during our time there as well. One woman had a husband that was called for a heart transplant while she and her veteran husband were at a check-up visit. We were able to see the joy and positive outcomes of more than a few patients while Rick was confined.

With Rick's health improving, Memorial Day of 2013 saw only slightly reduced duties on Rick's part at the VFW. His activity level with the LVAD dramatically increased. The shortness of breath doing small tasks such as walking more than a few feet was gone. Rick was healthy enough to participate in most of his VFW activities. In the same month, we made a visit to a local memorial hall and museum which honored area veterans. The organization created a walkway outside the building constructed with bricks honoring heroes of the military. Each brick displayed the name of the veteran with one of their military honors. We'd gotten the notice a brick for Rick was placed in the walkway. We made our way down the walkway reading bricks honoring the many military veterans. It was a surreal moment for us both as we approached the brick with Rick's name and the words *Bronze Star*.

The LVAD continued to work well and Rick's energy level increased week after week. We traveled across the state to a VFW convention. My VFW Ladies Auxiliary also participated in the convention. Rick received awards which included an All-State VFW commander's award. The summer progressed with no major LVAD issues. We awaited the six months follow-up visit to Richmond.

CHAPTER 10: Follow-up Visits & Life

While waiting at home for Rick's first follow-up visit to Richmond, our local Veterans hospital contracted with a non-veteran hospital in our area to handle LVAD emergency and immediate care in their LVAD clinic. My husband underwent cardiac rehabilitation three times a week at a local outpatient facility. I believe physical therapy helped tremendously in getting him back in healthy shape and tone. He had a significant weight loss when his illness peaked prior to the LVAD surgery. That summer was full of activities with family and VFW activities. Rick was well enough to participate in a neighborhood July 4th parade. I rode in an official car in the fourth of July parade with our Ladies Auxiliary for the first time.

We were excited and hoped that a donor heart would be available soon. It's difficult not to have mixed emotions about hoping for a matching donor heart to become available. We realize someone will lose their life for a continued life to be possible. Going through this process at this point made us realize the absolute necessity for organ donors.

In mid-August, we traveled to Richmond by plane for the first post-LVAD surgery follow-up. At the airport, we had the LVAD medical letter with us. The process of getting through the airport was much smoother this trip. However, the familiarity with the LVAD was still an issue with some of the airport staff we were in contact with.

Rick was admitted to the hospital for this short visit and I stayed at the Fisher House. Rick had various testing including imaging, x-rays and blood labs. Medication dosages were reviewed and changed as necessary. The LVAD speed was checked along with the controller operation. Any necessary adjustments to medication and the LVAD speed were made. Rick got a great checkup on that visit. We were told infection of the driveline site was one of the risks with an LVAD. Proper care had to be taken so the driveline wasn't pulled out of position. The area around the driveline had to be kept clean and changed regularly. During that visit, the LVAD nurses told me they were pleased with the condition of the driveline site on Rick's abdomen. I was glad for the nurses' compliment since I was a neophyte with this type of patient care. Rick was cleared to return home and follow-up back in Richmond in six months. We got the news shortly after this trip that Rick was put on the UNOS transplant list. His pressures and other criteria were met, and we'd now begin the official wait for a donor's heart. We packed *go bags* right away, so we'd be ready in case we got the call a donor's heart was found.

At the Fisher House on that follow-up visit, I met a few younger women house guests. The two women had husbands in active duty receiving treatment in the hospital. The spirit of the house hadn't changed since that initial stay six months prior. The checkup went wonderful and we returned home to continue our lives.

We were practically back to normal life in November 2013. Rick participated in a large Veterans Day parade with the VFW post. I was elated he had no CHF issues that plagued him before the LVAD. The difference in his energy level was remarkable at this point. With Rick's health drastically improving, I was able to look for full-time work again. It was a good time as any for a new career. The personal financial drain on household income and bills were significant. We were glad to have retirement funds saved to tide us through his illness. As a caregiver traveling back and forth out of the state with my husband, my employer couldn't be as flexible as I'd like. I understood my employer was running a business and had priorities. However, my place was with my husband and there was no mulling over that issue. We were grateful Rick's military service afforded him the healthcare resources he needed from the Veterans Administration. Most of the enormous medical expenses were taken care of which was a great blessing.

The flu season of late 2013 into 2014 was epic. I contracted the flu that season and it turned out to be the worse I'd had to date. Rick waited on me hand and foot while I was bedridden for longer than usual. The swine flu epidemic took more than a few lives in our area that year. We were glad Rick didn't contract it and was staying healthy. His immune system wasn't at its best and a virus would cause lots of issues with his health.

February of 2014 was the next post-LVAD follow-up visit to Richmond. That was a memorable trip, to say the least. Our flight to the connecting city of Philadelphia was slightly delayed and we missed our connecting flight to Richmond. We waited for hours but were eventually put on a later flight. This experience demonstrated the importance of carrying multiple LVAD batteries when traveling. Eventually, we were put on a later flight.

The medical checkup at the hospital in Virginia went well. Rick was progressing as expected with no issues. An ice storm was forecast and threatened to dump multiple inches of snow. Since Rick was doing so well, the LVAD nurse coordinators and support staff were great in helping us get the clearance to send Rick back home the next day after testing. Otherwise, we'd be stranded for several days which we weren't prepared for. Our home state wasn't forecast to get the storm until a day or two later. Our aunt was at home being looked after temporarily by my father while we were away. My father had health issues of his own during that time but was healthy enough to attend to his sister. We needed to get back home. Our flight arrangements were changed with the assistance of our local Veterans hospital travel department. We got a flight to the connecting city in North Carolina since there were no direct flights back to our city. Flights were getting grounded while we waited at the airport in Charlotte. Ultimately, our flight to our hometown was canceled. The airport customer service lines were packed with people trying to arrange alternative travel. We explained Rick's condition with the LVAD and the need to get home. After waiting a long while, an airport staff member got us on a flight to Philadelphia. The city was closer but still over three hundred miles away from our home. Of course, we took the flight and found out it was the last flight out before they were going to ground all future flights. We were exhausted by that point and thanking our lucky stars as well as the airport staff. The flight was packed. By the time we landed in Philadelphia, we were both exhausted since we'd been traveling close to half a day. We were told in Charlotte we could get a connecting flight home from Philadelphia the next day. We'd planned to try and make ourselves as comfortable as possible at the airport until the next morning's flight. Thank goodness we remembered to bring the battery charger for the LVAD! A silver lining when we got off the plane and went to the gate was an airline attendant with a clipboard. She asked our names, which we promptly gave. The airline employee told us we had a reservation at the airport hotel overnight. We were bowled over since it was a complete surprise. We assumed the attendant at the Charlotte airport setup the overnight accommodations as a courtesy with Rick's condition. Whatever the reason, we graciously accepted the reservations that were in our name and headed to the airport hotel. Whenever we talk about the experience, Rick and I agree life and people can surprise us in the most wonderful ways.

In the months that followed, the maintenance and routine of the LVAD had become comfortable for Rick. He only had a minor health issue since the last Richmond visit. We had a minor scare in the Spring after the February 2014 visit. Rick was congested and had trouble breathing one night. The LVAD monitor showed abnormal ranges on the various settings. He had to sit up in bed to sleep due to congestion making it difficult for him to lay flat.

The event scared us since some of the symptoms mimicked his pre-LVAD congestive heart failure. The one thing differentiating this from the congestive heart failure was Rick's sinus and nasal congestion. Thankfully, his physical symptoms turned out to be a sinus infection. He was back to normal in a short time. We were on alert that if any of the settings fell above or below the expected ranges, we'd call the LVAD coordinator day or night for assistance and direction. It was interesting to note how the LVAD settings varied when he was sick.

CHAPTER 11: 2014

The next follow-up in Richmond was August of 2014. It had

been eighteen months since the LVAD surgery. We'd heard and

read of some LVAD patients getting a donor heart before

eighteen months. Rick was healthy with the LVAD and we

didn't take it for granted. We knew in his case the next step was

a heart transplant, so we waited and hoped we'd get the call a

donor's heart was available. We flew south to Richmond toward

the end of August. On this trip, there were no available spaces at the Fisher House. I stayed at the same hospitality house as I did for Rick's evaluation in December of 2012. Rick was admitted as an inpatient for his testing during this visit. On designated follow-up visits Rick would get the heart catheterization procedure. One important thing the test would check for was the pulmonary pressures we already knew were a large concern with LVAD candidates.

Prior to the visit to Richmond in August 2014, there was a small concern about blood test results from his previous prostate screenings. Rick would routinely get the PSA (Prostate-Specific Antigen) screening done at our home clinic. The LVAD team in Richmond along with other medical specialty staff reviewed the previous lab results for the PSA screening while we were on this follow-up visit. Due to the abnormal values, additional screening was done while we were in Richmond. We were slightly worried initially since we were focused on my husband being as healthy as possible.

Our flight itinerary was for the usual two to three days depending on the testing schedule. By the second day, the coordinators told us we'd need to extend our visit. Although Rick appeared healthy, there were issues with something called the INR ratio in his blood on that visit. After the LVAD surgery, physicians prescribed blood thinners due to the risk of clotting. Rick was constantly monitored at our home clinic for the INR ratio. Depending on the results of the biweekly testing, the blood thinner medication was regulated. It was explained to us that blood could be either too thin or too thick. The INR ratio was carefully monitored. If the blood became too thin, there was a risk of bleeding. Conversely, thick blood would increase the risk of blood clots. With the issues of the INR and PSA values, our original departure date came and went.

After six days had passed, we were still in Richmond. I was at the hospitality house and Rick remained inpatient with various testing and regulation of his INR ratio. Due to lab test results, a prostate biopsy was recommended. If I'm thinking back correctly, the reason for waiting a few days to do the prostate biopsy was directly related to Rick's INR ratio. A higher risk of bleeding during the biopsy wasn't acceptable. Rick had a previous prostate biopsy with no issues in the past. I was informed by my husband he'd rather been shot again - as he'd been during his military service - than endure a prostate biopsy again. Rick said the biopsy was unimaginable pain. However, the biopsy needed to be done. It was close to a week into our stay in Richmond when I got word from the social worker at the hospital a room was available in the Fisher House. I remember getting ready that morning for my transportation to the hospital. After getting the good news about a room available, I rescheduled my transportation an hour or so ahead to allow me to pack. After checking in with the Fisher House to drop off my belongings, I headed to the Veterans hospital to visit with my husband.

I'm not sure of which day during our stay we'd met with several new specialists in Rick's room. However, I absolutely remember how I felt. Rick and I were in his hospital room and had visits by no less than three oncology staff members of different levels, experience, and title. The findings were that Rick had prostate cancer. Rick was silent only for a moment. His first question was about the treatment which would be determined when we met with the oncologist at home. The next question was about what the diagnosis meant for his LVAD and transplant status. We were told the LVAD team would speak with us about any changes. Rick was in *let's fix it* mode and ready to find out what the next step would be and what needed to be done.

After hearing the word *malignancy,* I remember feeling numb. We were suspicious this news would be the verdict since the events leading to this day were signaling some unknown issue. Rick and I talked about the possibility of malignancy only days before and tried to prepare ourselves. We hoped and prayed for the best. God doesn't give us more than we can handle, right?

My thoughts went to what my husband had been through with this heart issue over the years. I thought about the injuries in the military to his various body parts already healed from years ago. I wondered how my husband's body was going to handle any surgery or treatment for this cancer.

If I'm saying the word, *we* a lot in this book, it's because Rick

and I always talked in terms of what this journey would mean for

us. We travel, laugh, cry, and love together. We're a team and I

thank God every day for how we both love each other.

CHAPTER 12: Eyes on the Prize

We sat in the room for a few minutes after the specialist left. I don't remember crying in the room that day. The main thought in my mind was to keep on a strong face for my husband. He knew me well, though. He must have sensed I was on the verge of tears. Rick held my hand, looked me in the eyes and said, "We'll get through this."

"I know we will", I said.

The LVAD nurse coordinator we were familiar with for the past eighteen months came into the room. She was super supportive during the entire process before and after the LVAD surgery. The nurse asked us if our questions were answered by the specialists. We told her they gave us the general idea of his condition. We told her we realized follow-up and consult with the oncologist in our hometown was the next step. Once the coordinator was in the room, I think Rick and I were waiting for the answer to the questions we had in our mind. In retrospect, I believed she wanted to give us the news in the correct way by explaining things about the heart transplant list. She explained Rick wouldn't be taken off the heart transplant list. However, she stated he would now be inactive for a time on the list. The nurse went on to explain in detail how the inactive status would affect Rick's chances for a heart at this time. She explained that Rick would need to have the treatment for prostate cancer and be free of cancer for a time. However, the time he'd have to wait would depend on the results of the treatment and various other factors. She went on to say time already on the list would be considered whenever his status is changed. Having a malignancy and getting an LVAD isn't done as there are immunological concerns is what I remember hearing at that time. As a layperson, I understood logically since the immune system would be compromised with cancer treatment.

I couldn't believe what happened on this trip happened.

I felt so much for my husband and what he was going through. He was ready for the challenge, however. I noticed a change in his mindset. He was no longer focused on worrying about things we couldn't control. The focus was on getting home, meeting with the oncologists, and getting treatment for his condition. I envied him so much that day. His armor was on and he was ready for battle. Inside, I wanted to run screaming down the halls "why us, why him, why us!!" It would've been a great anecdote for this story, but I didn't do it. I took my husband's lead and remained calm. It wasn't easy to be calm and collected on that day. We prayed to God for strength as we sat in the room. Calm spirits and steadiness in mind were what we needed.

Our entire stay on that follow-up visit to Richmond was approximately twelve days. Rick was discharged from the hospital a day or two before our flight home. We got to enjoy the Fisher House while he was getting a few outpatient tests completed during the day. There were times I'd shed a tear and have my private pity parties. I'd felt we were so close to getting a heart for Rick (*of course I had no proof, but only hoped he was close to getting one by then*). After the diagnosis, we had no idea what the cancer treatment would be or how long it would take. I prayed about it and chose to look at the bright side: Rick was dealing with the news like a trooper, and the LVAD was functioning fine. We were up to the challenge. I figured if he's not freaking out, I shouldn't be either.

We arrived back home right before Labor Day. A get-together with family members at a local park that weekend was a welcome outing to the past weeks away from home. The oncology consult with the physician at the local Veterans hospital was informative. We got loads of reading material to supplement the verbal information we'd received from the oncologist and medical staff. It was decided radiation treatment was the best route. We were fortunate the malignancy wasn't worse and could be contained. There would be a minor procedure before the actual treatment.

In the meantime, I had my own issues with physical therapy for an acute back condition. Life eventually went back to normal for a short period of time. Rick was participating in a national VFW anniversary celebration being held in our town. I felt better and was back on my job hunt.

There was lots of anticipation about the radiation and any physical effects Rick would experience. I went with him for his first radiation treatment at the Veterans hospital. We could tell by the conversation of patients coming and going most were well into their treatments. The staff seemed to have a good rapport with the patients which made me feel comfortable. The first day went well and he was scheduled for more treatment throughout the week.

Rick did well with the treatments and had only minor side effects in those first weeks. I began working full-time later that month at a Veterans hospital facility across town. For some of his treatment schedule, Rick would ride with me in the morning to my work location. Shortly after we arrived at my work facility, he'd catch the Veterans hospital shuttle. The shuttle took veterans from one hospital location to another veterans' facility during the day. He'd then ride a shuttle back to my facility and wait until my shift was over. We'd drive home together.

After a while, Rick was exhausted with the additional traveling every day. There was no bus service in any proximity to where we lived. We tried for weeks to get Rick on a ride-sharing list for cancer patients going into the city. Our house was nearly thirteen miles from the Veterans facility where Rick received treatment. I worked outside the city in the opposite direction approximately twenty miles from our home. We were referred to different organizations providing rides for cancer patients to medical facilities. We were told our home location was in an area with few volunteers available to provide transportation service. I'd have to say The American Cancer Society worked hard to find us a driver in our area. A driver was eventually found for a few of

Rick's radiation treatments. After a short time, the volunteer was no longer available. We had to search again for new transportation to the scheduled treatments. We went back to our morning routine. I can't say it enough, Rick was a trooper. Eventually, we found another organization (Disabled American Veterans) servicing a couple of patients living five miles or so down the road. These patients were being transported to the same facility where Rick received his treatment. The days of the week he was able to ride the van was limited but was still helpful to us.

Of course, from this experience, we gained an even greater respect for the non-profit charitable organizations which help families in times of need. We gave back in the past, and we were happy to get help when we needed it. We found out lots of the people working for those organizations were volunteers. The selfless giving of others is what warms your heart during a health crisis or any other.

CHAPTER 13: Hurry Up and Wait

The new year of 2015 brought promise and hope as Rick toughed it out through his radiation treatment. There were moments where the physical side effects were a nuisance and sometimes an embarrassment for my husband. Those physical effects frustrated him, but he handled it alright. However, we kept saying out loud how blessed we were and how God had us in his hands.

Rick continued to do well and finished his course of radiation treatment by this first month of the year. January brought cold weather with school closings. Toward the end of the month, I came down with some type of respiratory issue lasting longer than normal. My husband soldiered on and drove me to work on the snow days.

February brought much of the same weather as the previous month in that year. I documented several pictures of my travels in the snow going to and from home during the month. We both spent more time with the local grandkids, and they continued to keep us feeling young. We were anxious to get back to Richmond for a follow-up visit for the LVAD. Rick was at the two-year mark for getting the LVAD implanted. The LVAD was working fine all during Rick's three-month treatment. He got glowing reports from the local oncology and medical physicians. Our normal six-month visit to Richmond couldn't happen due to the cancer treatment. Rick was going to be seen at the LVAD clinic later in the spring. We looked forward to the trip and hoped to get back on track with his bridge to transplant path.

May of 2015 was a busy month. We had a larger than normal get

together with family and friends on Rick's birthday. I decided to

get mostly pre-cooked food since working and making sure my

aunt's needs were taken care of took most of my time. Rick

continued to take great care of auntie during the day when I

worked. The LVAD checkup in Richmond was scheduled toward

the end of the month. We hadn't been to Richmond since the

previous summer. From what I recall, the visit was typical with

the normal diagnostic tests for the heart and lung functions.

Unfortunately, we knew the wait for a heart would be longer due

to his treatments. We were told clearance from oncologists and

cardiac staff would be needed. The wait continued. Patience was

a virtue we had to embrace throughout the entire process. I

believe it was the hardest during this time. This roadblock of

sorts served to test our resolve even more.

The summer of 2015 was mostly non-eventful as far as health

issues. We went about our lives almost as normal. We decided to

go to an outdoor concert by a long-time favorite singer of mine,

Natalie Cole. This concert ended up being one of the singer's last concerts leading to her death at the end of the year. The normality in our lives was a good thing. The wound dressings at the site, controller module checks, and battery changes had become routine things we did at home.

By the time late September arrived, I was ready for a low-key birthday celebration with Rick. My own medical issues were becoming acute, but nothing on the scale of Rick's condition. There was great news of my daughter expecting twins. With two girls already, the new addition of twins would expand her family from four to six. In early November, we took a weekend trip across the state to see the other grandchildren on Rick's side of the family. Rick's daughter had four children he'd never seen in person. They'd previously lived in another state close to a thousand miles away and we only saw pictures of the grandchildren. Thankfully, they now resided in Rick's hometown less than a few hundred miles away. We needed this trip to happen. The unknown of Rick's long-term prognosis was weighing on us both. I personally felt he needed the morale booster no matter the brave face he was wearing throughout. We made the weekend trip in early November. The four children were all under seven years old and knew Rick as Pop-Pop. It was a beautiful reunion. Rick admitted to me as we traveled back home that weekend, he was so happy we made the trip.

Later that month, my husband and I were able to enjoy a weekend getaway for our wedding anniversary. The holidays were happy and fulfilling as we spent time with family. My own personal medical conditions came to a head and we had a serious talk about my continuing to work. The multitude of diagnostics tests I needed as well as my acute physical conditions made Rick my caregiver for a short time.

The New Year of 2016 came in with a bang with my favorite sports team, the Pittsburgh Steelers, going to the playoffs. We lost the AFC divisional football game to the Denver Broncos, but I noted to myself and anyone interested our team went out like champs and left it all on the field. By that time, I'd resigned from my job to focus on my health and continue to be a support for my husband.

Rick's next medical LVAD check-up in Richmond was scheduled for March of 2016. It was a promising trip and a good checkup for Rick. We came back home from Virginia and life went on as usual. Our two grandchildren living near our town were doing ballet recitals and we got to see their performances that month. We had to reconcile within ourselves more time had to past in his cancer recovery before he'd have a chance of donor's heart. We were consigned to hurry up and wait.

CHAPTER 14: Trials & Tribulations

As Spring 2016 approached, Rick was having a few medical issues. Around the same time, we lost my daughter's mother-in-law to illness. Rick and I attended the memorial service for support of our memory to her and our extended family. During the service, Rick had a medical emergency and we had to race to the hospital. He was monitored in the emergency room and the LVAD controller *seemed* to be working correctly. The LVAD had been implanted for three years and we'd had no major issues prior to this point in time. His condition stabilized, and we looked to the future.

During that same time period, our blended family expanded with new babies being born on both sides. My daughter's twin baby girls living in our area were important in the healing process for us both. The saying grandchildren can keep you feeling young rang true for us. The following month of May was a whirlwind and surreal in many ways. Our two new grandbabies were filmed for a scene in a major motion picture filmed in our city.

Around this time, my dad was rushed to the hospital and only days later diagnosed with an advanced form of cancer. Rick was having some medical issues not related to his LVAD. I didn't know if I was coming or going. My dad's illness wasn't expected or even known by the family to my knowledge. I have to say I'd never seen such grace and acceptance with death before my father's illness. My father talked with the palliative care physicians and professionals at the hospital during his stay. The main thing my father questioned was what he should expect when he was transitioning from this world. I remember being in the room when the physician told my dad he would be made as comfortable as possible. My dad's wishes were for no extraordinary measures to be performed to keep him alive. He wasn't interested in chemotherapy or any treatments which he felt would lessen his quality of life. My dad said to me, "Baby, we all got to leave here sometime." He said he wanted me to make sure he passed on the way he wanted. It's hard not to be selfish when we're losing a loved one. In the end, I believe honoring wishes of the dying is sacred – no matter how we, the living, feel on the subject.

One day on a visit with my father in the hospital, I watched him think Rick for as he put it, "taking care of my daughter." I couldn't hold back the tears. When we were notified my dad was getting worse, family and a few friends gathered around his hospital bed late on a Sunday evening. My dad was at peace. We sang gospel songs around Dad's bed as he transitioned from this life. On his last breaths, I was at my dad's side holding his hand.

My dad had his children, brothers, sisters, grandchildren, other family members, and a dear friend at his side.

The family was devastated by my dad's sudden death. My dad was only hospitalized for a couple of weeks before his death. Rick and I had the responsibility of clearing Dad's apartment and making funeral arrangements. There was little time to mourn. Both my husband and I went into auto-pilot mode. We were thankful for a few helpful family members assisting Rick with most of the heavy work in my father's apartment. My stepbrother went above and beyond helping with the physical work. He made sure Rick didn't overexert himself. Of course, Rick ended up doing too much physically, his usual way of doing things.

The following month of June brought new challenges for my aunt living in our home. An emergency trip to the hospital revealed she needed surgery for a large hernia she'd had for years. Auntie's surgery went well but the hospital stay was longer than normal for her condition. Multiple blood transfusions were done during her stay to stabilize her condition. She was discharged home to us for care at home. Rick seemed worse for the wear by that time.

The next month of July brought on more things to keep us busy and remind us that we were alive. We relocated to be closer to the Veterans hospital for Rick's care as well as the grandchildren living in our town. We were smart enough to get professional movers, but there were personal items we moved on our own. Our previous townhome was a large three-story space. The task of clearing the huge full basement fell to us since those items needed to be in storage. The new place was larger, but we had lots of things we didn't or couldn't part with. I must make a point that before the LVAD, most of the physical things Rick did in those few months in 2016 wouldn't have been possible.

CHAPTER 15: The Turning Point

The move back to the busy city was more mentally exhausting than physically. The townhouse was large and had over seventeen hundred square feet of space. There was the challenge of steps, however. In the new place, there were two sets of steps from the street area leading to the front door. One short set to get to the walkway, and another short set of concrete steps to get to our door. The front door opened into a small area at the bottom of the carpeted stairs. The full flight of stairs had at least sixteen steps. The living room area was huge and had a dining room area with ceiling fan off to the side. The kitchen was small compared to our previous one. The kitchen was a walk-in type. The counter space was minimal and something I wasn't used to for a long time. Auntie wasn't happy with all the steps with her chronic arthritis. We both knew we didn't think the move through. Since we'd given notice at our previous townhome, we were expected to move so we had to follow through. The convenient location in the city couldn't be beaten, however.

One night about a few weeks after moving into the new place, Rick's LVAD controller alarm sounded. We were asleep when the alarm went off. What we thought about only in the back of our minds, was now a reality. We sat up in bed feeling startled as we inspected the LVAD controller attached to Rick. The alarm type was one we knew meant our next act would be to get to a hospital emergency department. The LVAD was plugged into a/c power as usual when Rick slept. We immediately changed and put in fresh batteries for the LVAD, got dressed and headed for the hospital. We went to the local commercial hospital designated for emergency LVAD issues. The hospital had a heart transplant and LVAD program. Rick was now having some of his outpatient follow-up care at this local commercial hospital. We didn't have to worry about any additional expenses at the commercial hospital. The non-Veteran Administration care was covered under Rick's benefits.

The sounding of this alarm was a first for us in the entire three years since the LVAD implantation surgery. I was a nervous wreck inside. We both knew if the LVAD failed, it was a life-threatening event for Rick. His heart would be too weak to sustain him for very long, so we knew the alarm sounding was a serious issue.

After arriving at the hospital, we explained what happened with the LVAD. The hospital staff was familiar with the device and called the cardiac team for the examination. The usual vitals and blood labs were taken to assess Rick's condition. After a couple of hours or more, we were told the manufacturer of the LVAD needed more time to assess the error message on the LVAD controller. The emergency department physicians and LVAD technical support had to wait for an answer from the LVAD manufacturer. We could only assume at the late hour no one was available at the manufacturer's facility or office to give direction on how to clear or stop the error message. The blessing was Rick's vitals were fine even with the alarm sounding. What we were afraid of was the LVAD function since the error message was one of the fatal errors signaling something was wrong with the unit.

After some time on this first emergency room visit for the controller alarm, the in-house LVAD engineers at the hospital were able to reset the controller. The controller appeared to be working normally and Rick was discharged from the emergency room to home. A weight was lifted from us on that day. Because of Rick's great progress and success with the LVAD, we were expecting only great things until a donor's heart was received. We breathed a sigh of relief.

The days that followed brought more than a few repeats of that first night when the LVAD controller alarm went off. The alarms went off more than a few times over the week. We had to rush to the emergency room each time the controller unit alarm sounded and displayed the error message. After a few visits from us, the hospital got a spare LVAD controller unit and switched it with Rick's original unit.

Finally, after so many visits to the emergency room for alarms still going off, the out-of-town manufacturer sent a technician to look at the failing LVAD controllers. We had no other option at that point. Changing controllers was obviously not a solution to our problem. The LVAD was implanted but if the device monitoring its efficiency was defective, we couldn't be certain how Rick would be affected. We needed to find out more before we could feel comfortable. The LVAD team in Richmond was notified of the issue early on.

In addition to the LVAD issues during that time, my aunt was having medical issues again. Rick needed to be hospitalized since the medical staff cautioned the LVAD unit was malfunctioning. My aunt was hospitalized at another hospital concurrently with Rick's admission. I could do nothing but pray. My activities were going back and forth to both hospitals checking on my husband and aunt.

Finally, on the day in August 2016, it was decided that Rick needed to be sent back to Richmond from the local hospital. In the event of a malfunction requiring a replacement of the LVAD, open-heart surgery would be necessary. The surgeons in Richmond would be the ones to perform the surgery – the team which implanted the device. The decision was made for emergency transport to the Richmond Veteran's hospital. Rick was transported by air ambulance from the intensive care unit of the local hospital. The ICU was where Rick needed to be, as the malfunction of the LVAD was considered a life-threatening condition.

It was difficult to make the decision to stay behind while Rick went on the air ambulance from the hospital that day. I knew my place was with him in this emergency. However, my aunt was in our care and we were her caregivers. Rick and I agreed I needed to stay and get things situated with our Aunt. She was still in the hospital with no apparent discharge date.

I prayed God would keep Rick safe and I'd be able to see him again. This was all so scary. Again, mental auto-pilot mode was needed to cope. After a couple of days checking on auntie and getting things situated at the new townhome, I needed to take the long drive to Richmond. We'd only lived in the new townhouse for a few weeks. I packed lots of clothing since we had no idea how long Rick would be in the Richmond hospital.

My daughter took on the task of coordinating our aunt's discharge from the hospital. I had to get on the road. I remember being more exhausted than I'd ever been in my life. The prior week's events and lack of sleep had my own health suffering. I had to make mental and hardcopy notes to remind me to take medications. It's easy to get off track when things are going haywire. I found I had to set an alarm on my cellphone to remind me to take my most important medication, a blood pressure pill.

There was nothing except God watching over me during those days. I look back and know I didn't get through those days alone. I had to prepare for the long drive to Richmond to get to my husband. I had no idea what was going on with the medical investigation of the LVAD problem. From the little I understood, the staff was at a loss with this kind of LVAD malfunction.

CHAPTER 16: Drive

I had the car packed in anticipation of a long stay in Richmond. Of course, I had no idea how long we'd be away from home. The consensus was that no one knew at the time. I remember the day I left on the drive to Richmond vividly. I had my departure time planned and the West Penn Auto Club paper maps were on hand for the drive. The car was stocked with supplies for the road. I'd planned only fifteen-minute rest breaks. My experience driving long distances in the past was I did well with short rest breaks. The constant stopping and relaxing at a rest stop when traveling on my own wasn't something I enjoyed.

The first rest stop was non-eventful and only about an hour into the drive. I stayed with my schedule and stopped for a short break. I had food and water in the car and was good to go. The next rest stop went as planned. I played music in the car as usual while singing along as I always do. The third rest stop came between two and two and a half hours of driving. I decided to sit and get a bite to eat quickly, even though I had some snack food in the car. I ended up checking email and phone messages at the rest stop and relaxing (something I'd planned on not doing). Before I knew it, over forty-five minutes had passed. I was close to an hour behind on my drive.

I got back on the road determined to take only short breaks again to finish the additional three hours of driving. After another hour or so of driving, I had to use a rest stop. I'm sure my bladder was getting back at me for all the pressure of holding it for long periods of time. In any case, as I drove up to the rest stop, my bladder released, and I was mortified as well as upset. The rest stop was one of the smaller stops with only restrooms and a couple of outdoor vending machines. However, the stop was busy with people coming and going. I wasn't going to get out of the car visibly soaked to change clothes. In retrospect, I probably should have gotten out of the car no matter the embarrassment. I wanted to get to Rick as soon as I could. The mental exhaustion was taking its toll and I wasn't making logical decisions. I've learned my lesson about testing an aging bladder. I'm sure stress played a large part, as well.

I remember being upset, crying and mad at myself at the same time. I was mad for not stopping sooner and trying to stick to such an unrealistic schedule. I was upset about feeling so helpless where my aunt and Rick were concerned. I cried because I think everything that happened recently had me so shell-shocked, I didn't have time to realize things *might* get worse before they got better.

The reservations were made for the hospitality house in Richmond due to short notice and no availability at the Fisher House. I arrived at the downtown hospitality house in the late afternoon. There wasn't on-site parking and guests were expected to park in the front area no more than fifteen minutes to load or unload cars. As I walked from the car to the front door of the house, I got a whiff of the urine-soaked skirt I was wearing. Embarrassment was no longer a factor since I'd done loads of crying and feeling sorry on the long drive down.

I remember purposely holding my head up high while checking into the hospitality house with the front desk staff. I asked about the parking situation. The previous times we were here, I didn't have a need for parking. We'd usually fly and would have complimentary transportation to and from the Veterans hospital. The desk staff person gave me two options. I could go down the block to a parking garage or park for free at the downtown university about a five-minute drive away. If I chose to park at the university, a shuttle was available to transport me back. I informed the hospitality house staff person I'd move the car as soon as I got the luggage in my room and freshened up.

The next hour in my room was spent showering and decompressing. I didn't worry about the fifteen-minute parking limit. I talked with Rick and he was relieved I arrived safely. I told him about my travel debacle on the interstate. With a migraine and exhaustion threatening to knock me down, I went back to the lobby since I needed to move the car. The desk clerk gave me a card with the shuttle telephone number since I said I'd park at the university. I wasn't in the mood to walk to a garage in the evening alone looking like an easy target for someone up to no good. I'd have no problem in the same situation in familiar surroundings. From a previous visit, I was aware of a shuttle running from the hospitality house to the university hospital but never had to use the service. I assumed the shuttle was still running at the time I arrived. I figured I'd park at the university garage and wait and get the shuttle on its next run.

The drive to the university hospital garage was hairy because I got confused about the route. I drove on a few wrong streets but finally found the hospital. I suddenly realized I didn't know which garage I needed to park in to catch the shuttle back to the hospitality house. The evening was progressing, but it wasn't dusk yet since it was late August.

I drove near the university hospital and saw a man with a security guard's uniform standing at a corner. The corner was near a street leading to the hospital's emergency room entrance. I pulled the car around the corner on the short driveway leading to the emergency room. I'd hope to go around the circular driveway and be on my way after I received directions. I rolled the driver's side window down said to the security guard standing in the street near the curb, "Excuse me, I need to get to the garage to park and catch the shuttle to the hospitality house. Can you tell me where I need to park?"

"Lady, I don't know what you're talking about. You need to back up here and try not to hit anybody and go up that way," said the snarky self-important security officer.

I looked at him as if he had two heads and was confused as to what I'd said so wrong to receive such a rude response.

"Back up", he repeated as if he were scolding me.

Considering my line of sight was blocked, I wasn't going to back the car into the street traffic. Additionally, I wanted to show him I could care less about what he said because he said it so rudely. *Wasn't he hired to be a little helpful?* I thought to myself. In any case, I didn't back the car up. I drove around the emergency room entrance and past the main entrance. Before I got out of the other end of the driveway, a uniformed sheriff was walking toward the hospital main entrance. I opened my window and asked him the same question I'd asked the security officer a few minutes earlier. The sheriff politely said he wasn't sure since he's coming in from another county to pick someone up. However, the nice sheriff told me he knew of a garage further up the street and one with an entrance directly around the corner. He said he was sorry he couldn't be more of help.

I drove my car further down the block and a rush of emotion overtook me. I was exhausted, having respiratory issues and upset at the entire day's events. My asthma, anxiety, exhaustion, and frustration got the best of me and I felt I needed to pull the car over. Considering I didn't know where I was going, I decided to pull over to a curb. The over three-hundred-mile drive and total exhaustion took its toll on all my senses. I shed some tears of frustration for a few minutes more before I called Rick. I wanted to compose myself and didn't want him to worry. Rick told me to call the hospitality house again and have them explain exactly where I needed to go. My husband knew I wanted to try and figure everything out for myself as usual. He wanted me to call him back after I got the car to the garage. He could tell I wasn't completely myself and I was at a breaking point. Yes, he needed to hold my hand on this one since I was stressed and in physical distress. I'd been the caregiver and strong rock for everyone for so long this mini meltdown had to occur at some point. That day was as good a time as any. I'd wish I'd been safe and alone in my room, but the meltdown was inevitable and necessary. I cry when I'm upset and angry. I get strength in the aftermath of both emotions.

When I called the hospitality house from the car, I was told the garage I needed to park the car was located next to the hospital. The hospitality house staff person also told me I needed to call the shuttle since they only ran on a per-call basis after a certain time – a fact I would've loved to have known earlier. I didn't remember the desk clerk mentioning I needed to call for the shuttle when I checked in at the hospitality house. Honestly, with all the emotions going on during the day, she may have mentioned it and I didn't hear it when I checked in at the desk. After getting more clear directions, I drove around the surrounding streets of the university buildings and made my way to the hospital's garage. I noticed this lot was on the opposite side of the emergency room entrance where I was earlier. I had no idea I was so close to the lot when I first arrived at the university hospital.

After driving into the lot, I saw a parking lot attendant standing on the upper outside deck. I gave him the same spiel about wanting to catch the shuttle. I was confident I was in the right place. I asked the lot attendant where the shuttle pickup spot was located. The man wasn't rude but told me he worked here for a long time and didn't know of a shuttle. I parked anyway and called the shuttle after-hours service number. I was told a driver was out near my location and would be at the hospital shortly. I parked and called Rick to tell him the car and myself were safe and I was waiting for the shuttle. I apologized for scaring him. Sometimes, a person needs a friendly face and a nice gesture when they're on the edge. Thankfully, the worse of the day had already happened.

After parking, I high tailed it up the parking ramp. I thought I'd pass out since my lungs felt like they were tightening. As I reached the top of the ramp, a white shuttle-type van drove in on the top ramp. As he passed me, he stopped the van and called my last name. I was so relieved the nightmare of a day was almost over.

Back at the hospitality house, I headed straight to the elevator. I was glad to be back in my room. Exhaustion took its toll on me and all I wanted was a good night's sleep. After calling Rick and telling him I was safe and sound in the room, I was ready to pass out. I slept for nine hours until morning. I'm still hard-pressed to remember the last time I got nine hours of sleep. Apparently, the increased level of stress and exhaustion forced my body to heal a little.

Thankfully, I remembered the night before to call and order the transportation to the hospital in the morning. The Veterans hospital used a transportation company to transport guests staying downtown out to their facility on the south side of town. The transportation company wasn't connected with the shuttle service going to the university hospital. Special travel vouchers were needed for transport to the Veterans hospital from the hospitality house. I'd get the vouchers on my first day visiting the hospital. The social worker assigned to Rick's case provided the preapproved vouchers. The transport arrived on time the morning after my nine-hour sleep and was filled with people as usual. I was excited as I traveled in the van to see my husband at the hospital. He had a few days of being alone and away from home in a hospital with no family. When we arrived at the hospital, I called Rick from the lobby to tell him I'd be on his floor in a few minutes. As I rounded the corner in his unit, I saw him standing in the hall waiting for me. Talk about a sight for sore eyes!

CHAPTER 17: Settling In

After a few days, I got word my aunt would be discharged from the hospital in our hometown. I coordinated her care with my daughter and the hospital staff. She was going to need placement in a long-term skilled facility. She still needed skilled care and couldn't live at home on her own. I was glad to know she would be taken care of until we returned home. The hope was she'd get the care she needed at the nursing facility while we were away.

The saga with finding out what was happening with the LVAD continued. Rick was confined to his floor for safety reasons in case of an issue with the LVAD. He loved to walk around various parts of the hospital on his previous inpatient stays. However, due to the volatile situation with the controller alarms, the medical staff was being cautious. He needed to be in the vicinity of the nursing floor in case he needed medical assistance. The first two months away from home during this stay were hard for us both. Rick was always so independent and was going stir crazy not knowing how the issue with the LVAD alarms would be resolved. We hoped the donor heart would be found soon. During this time in the Fall of 2016, Rick was past the three-and-a-half-year mark of LVAD implantation.

A month into our stay, one of my first cousins back home passed away. She and I always got along so well. We'd see each other sporadically throughout the years. Our talks on the phones lasted for hours when they happened. My cousin was only a few years older than me. Her illness was news to me. By the time I heard of her condition, she was critical in the hospital.

I prayed so much for Rick's strength, mine and everyone concerned. I also prayed the medical staff would have a solution to why the LVAD seemed to be failing Rick. His physical condition was good. However, if the LVAD shut down, he'd need medical assistance immediately. It was working for his heart. The unknown is sometimes scary.

Sometime in the first couple of weeks, a spot opened at the Fisher House. One morning when I was getting ready to visit Rick, the social worker from the Veterans hospital called and informed me a room at the Fisher House was waiting for me. I was again grateful to be closer in the vicinity to Rick, especially if an emergency would happen. A cab ride to the other side of town wasn't a reliable option either. I had good and bad experiences with cab service on a previous visit. The Fisher House was still my home away from home and I felt more comfortable each time I stayed as a guest. Rick said he was happy about me getting the room at the Fisher House. His mind was more at ease knowing I wasn't downtown in an area known as unsafe at times.

Some of the pleasant things that happened on that stay in Richmond was the kind and helpful people we met along the way. The women and men police officers we met at the Veterans hospital seemed very dedicated to their work. One of the awesome officers we met was a kind and friendly soul who went above and beyond during our stay. I remember my first encounter with the officer at the Fisher House. I was talking with a group of guests in the kitchen area. The police officer was walking rounds and wanted to know if everyone was doing alright. People were discussing baking and birthday cakes. I mentioned my birthday was coming up in a few weeks. The officer mentioned his wife baked cakes. After a few weeks, I hadn't seen the officer since that first day in the kitchen. It was now the day following my birthday and I was in my room relaxing after dinner. I received a text from a house guest who I'd become acquainted with at the house. The house guest's text informed me someone left a cake for me in the kitchen. I was pleasantly surprised, thankful, and overwhelmed when I opened the box with the cake. The gift and gesture raised my spirits as I shared the cake with the house guests that evening. I called Rick's hospital room and told him about the cake. My husband asked me to give the officer his thanks for lifting my spirits. I was blessed to witness this same officer's acts of kindness and generosity to many others over the months of our stay in Richmond.

Later the same evening, while back in my room, the same house guest I'd received a text from earlier, texted me again. The text informed me one of the newer house guests left a music cd out front in the common area for me. It was another birthday gift for me which made me realize I was surrounded by kind and supportive people. Those are only a couple of stories of many kindnesses received during our long stay in Richmond. On the same night, the woman who sent me the text also wrote in another text, "See you're special and don't even know it." I remember smiling and feeling blessed when I read the text.

After a while, Rick felt he needed to spread his wings. He needed to get out of the confines of the walls of his private hospital room. Rick was starting to feel more comfortable venturing further away from his room. Because he had to keep a telemetry monitor attached to his body, he needed to inform the nursing staff if he was traveling off the floor. The staff could place the monitor on a standby mode until he returned. I could tell my husband was getting restless those first few months of his stay as an inpatient. Rick needed to get off the nursing floor for his sanity. He would sometimes get scolded by the staff for leaving the floor without notifying anyone. One of my husband's sayings is, "I've been chewed out before." I can't imagine how hard it was for him to be stifled in his movements and activity. We knew the rules were for his health should something go wrong with the LVAD. We're fortunate nothing serious happened in his ventures away from the unit. I believe there was a higher power watching us from the beginning.

CHAPTER 18: Explorations

After about three months, it was my turn to get stir crazy. I knew worrying constantly wasn't doing me any favors. I had the car handy on this trip and felt the need to explore. I'd only been to a few familiar places since I'd arrived. My shopping was done no more than seven or eight miles from the Veterans hospital. There were food and clothing shopping areas much closer to the hospital as well. Someone back home suggested maybe getting out and exploring would be a great thing to keep my mind occupied. They were right. I decided to visit a couple of new shopping centers I hadn't got the chance to visit on our last trip. I gained confidence in my knowledge of the area as the weeks passed.

Every morning, my morning routine went as follows: I'd get up and have breakfast in the dining room. I'd make another pot of coffee for the house kitchen, if necessary. The early morning risers would usually deplete the first pot. Other house guests and I would set the coffee pot on an early morning timer the night before. After breakfast, I'd return to my room and get ready to go to the hospital. I'd usually relax in the room keeping myself busy reading or watching the morning news report for a while. I never wanted to visit before regular visiting hours unless there was an issue with Rick. There were morning routine activities the medical staff had for Rick I didn't want to disturb. Time to relax in the morning was important to me as well.

One morning, the local news morning talk show had local authors on the broadcast. The authors talked about a writer's festival being held at a location outside of the city. I mapped the location and found it wasn't too far from a shopping area I'd recently visited. The festival was being held at a library. The panelist on the show had an interesting talk about a book. I told myself, this was my opportunity to do something I enjoyed. I'd written in diaries and journals for most of my life. During my childhood, I'd write stories and poems for fun. I wrote a collection of poems and flash fiction years before. The collection was published by a small press as a chapbook. I wanted to learn about some of the local writers and how they began their careers. Rick's heart issues made me know I needed to get writing again. I had journals and online blogs, but I wasn't consistent with my writing at that point. I told Rick about the writer's festival and he was glad I wanted to get out and explore. I believe he could sense my need to do something I enjoyed. I assured my husband I'd be careful venturing further out on my own and would check in with him.

The event happened on a Saturday. Rick was ready to go to a recreational cornhole event with the other patients at the hospital. The event was being held in a large activity room at the hospital. I was glad Rick would be occupied with something other than sitting in the hospital room.

The GPS directions didn't fail me on the trip outside of town to the festival. I arrived at the time I expected. I was able to get a decent parking spot and saw that people were gathered to go into the library for the event. I'd planned to go to an author's reading and visit the various tables set up for the event. My arrival was right on time since the room for the author's reading filled up quickly. The author came into the room and introduced herself. She had a few slides and explained her book. The book gave an account of her southern hometown history from years ago with school desegregation. The book detailed the events of how the public schools were closed to prevent desegregation. Black children were denied an education for a time. The story was an interesting one that I hadn't heard about in any history lesson.

There were a couple of older people in the room that remembered this event when they were younger. One of the audience members had a relative that used to talk about the events during that time. I was happy I went and got to hear the author and the other personal accounts.

After the author spoke, I made my way to her table out on the library floor and purchased the book. I was able to get a signed copy and had a short conversation with the author. A lunch stand was set up outside by a local vendor. I purchased a bag lunch and found a nearby table outside the library. There were other writers at the table. Mostly everyone had a business card and was a published author. I enjoyed the interesting conversation with the authors. The group at the table was an eclectic mix of ages. After lunch, I returned to the library to browse the other offerings of interest. There was a musician playing folk music on a guitar well. An employee was giving information about the upcoming events at the library. I found out about a 3D printing class that was being held in the coming weeks. The staff member had a small model of an action figure that was made on the printer. I was interested but didn't make it back to the library to try the 3D printing myself. All in all, it was a great day out alone. I talked about it for a few days to anyone who'd listen.

CHAPTER 19: Holidays

The holidays were approaching, and Rick and I realized we'd
most likely be away from home by the time Thanksgiving
arrived. We wanted to be home but knew that the best place for
Rick with the issues going on would be at the hospital.
Thanksgiving for us was always a holiday to reconnect with
family. Most of the holiday celebrations we had at home were
filled with food, laughter and enjoying family. We knew that the
holidays would be difficult.

Thankfully, the Veterans hospital and Fisher House staff provide lots of support to the veterans and their families all year round. The holidays are a special time at the hospital and the Fisher House. Many volunteer organizations provide guests with holiday meals. Certain staff members also took it upon themselves to provide guests with holiday meals from their personal expenses. I found I needed to experience being with others not as fortunate to realize how blessed Rick and I were. I thought I knew how blessed we were, but I didn't.

Thanksgiving Day at the Fisher House was wonderful and filled with helpful volunteers giving their time and caring. Rick was able to eat a regular diet, so I made sure he had a nice helping of the food he loves so much. Turkey and all the trimmings including desserts and soft drinks were in abundance. I felt thankful for being there and didn't worry about my troubles too much or, at all during that time.

I made a few connections with the guests of the Fisher House. There were several spouses of LVAD patients I was fortunate to meet. We shared different experiences as caregivers but were the same since we all had a veteran spouse needing acute care in the hospital.

One woman staying in the house was an acquaintance from a visit a couple of years before when Rick was receiving his LVAD. She stayed in the house while her husband underwent a surgical procedure on his heart. I remember her having issues with her employer about when she was returning to work. The return to work issue for employed caregivers was a common theme for both men and women caregivers I'd met at the time. For those of us not retired, being away from the job caused issues as time passed. I'd experienced the same issues with an employer more than reasonable about my initial time away from the job. However, as time goes on, most employers aren't as reasonable. The Family Medical Leave Act (FMLA) was used by more than a few caregivers I'd met in Richmond. I used the benefit of FMLA during Rick's LVAD surgery hospital stay. The weeks off from work used toward the FMLA can dwindle right before your eyes. The woman I mentioned above struggled with the decision of whether to take a more permanent leave from the job or return to her job. This woman and her husband lived a couple of hundred miles away from the Richmond hospital. The stress of trying to keep up your livelihood and being a support to a spouse or loved one is a difficult thing to manage.

Another woman I met had a husband in the hospital for an injury. She didn't have any outside work concerns but had enough worries to keep her busy. Her husband had progressed to the point where he was to be discharged in another month or so. Her concerns were getting their home updated for the equipment her husband would need in their home. She stayed at her husband's side in the hospital from early morning to late in the evening. I admired her physical and mental strength. Family members of patients with spinal cord injuries played a more hands-on role during their loved one's care. I remember this woman being up by dawn to eat breakfast. She'd go to the hospital to assist with getting her husband ready for his different therapies. I'd witness her return late in the evenings to the Fisher House.

Another woman I met was the family member of a younger veteran that was injured. The young veteran had multiple traumas and had been recuperating for several months when I met her on this stay at the Fisher House. She also played an active role as a caregiver for her family members. She would stay most of the day with her relative who was confined to a wheelchair and had neurological challenges. Her relative had to learn to walk and speak again. I have to say noticing the young man's progress was an example of only one of the many miraculous things I'd seen during my stay at the hospital campus. This woman would tell the story of this young veteran often. She'd tell of how he was injured overseas and brought back to the United States to another Veterans hospital. The young veteran was one of many in the same situation at the hospital from what I understood. The woman said her relative was critical during the first two months after his injury but got through the first hurdle. This young veteran wasn't expected to live in the first month the woman would explain when she told the story. He could barely move and couldn't talk she explained. This woman would say, "but God had other plans for him and brought him a long way." When her family member got well enough, the woman would bring him to the Fisher House for an hour or so to sit and watch television. He was unable to talk clearly, but this woman seemed to understand everything he was trying to say. What a faithful support she was to her family member. We should all have people in our lives willing to go the distance when we're in need. By the time the young man was to be transferred to a rehabilitation facility closer to his home state, he was standing for a few minutes at a time. I marveled at the progress I'd seen with my eyes and the greatness of the power of love and the human spirit.

I met a woman whose husband had an LVAD but had severe medical issues. He was a bit older than my middle-aged husband. This woman said she believed in the power of prayer. Her husband was critical at one point but pulled through. He received a heart transplant during my stay there. I was so happy to see someone else get the gift of life. In these situations, you can only rejoice about God's glory when you see a life saved. The skilled surgeons and medical staff that save lives daily are a special breed. Shortly after this retired veteran's heart transplant, he got gravely ill. It was touch and go for a time, but this woman said she'd put it in God's hands. Her husband pulled through and was on the road to recovery during the holiday season.

I met another woman at the Fisher House closer to my age. Her husband was suffering from severe CHF and needed an LVAD. The veteran was reluctant to get the surgery out of fear which was understandable. The prognosis was dire for this veteran without surgical intervention. One evening when I was leaving the hospital, she saw me get off the elevator on the ground floor. She asked me if I had time to talk with her husband about the LVAD. I told her I'd help in any way I could. Her husband was in the ICU and I can recall how difficult it was for him to speak without sounding like he was out of breath. This man's condition reminded me of how Rick was during the time he was critical in our local hospital before the LVAD surgery. The woman explained to her husband I was the wife of a veteran who had the LVAD implanted. I told the man I'd answer any questions that I could. I spoke to the man briefly with his wife in the intensive care unit. I called Rick's room to let the man speak with him on the phone that evening. Rick also agreed to visit the man sometime the next day to speak with him personally. The wife said she'd run out of options trying to convince her husband the LVAD surgery was what would give him a chance at a longer life together. She said she could see her husband was fighting for his life and wanted to do everything in her power to help him. I told her the surgery was a personal decision and to make sure to ask the medical staff lots of questions. The next day, Rick was able to speak with the man in person and explain what the LVAD did for him. I believe Rick could've been an official spokesman for this device when he explained how it saved his life. Rick talked about how his own physical health had improved after the surgery. He told the man how he walked every day and had lots of energy. I was so proud of the way my husband helped the man understand his experience with the LVAD. The man eventually had the LVAD surgery. The woman's husband wasn't the first patient Rick spoke to about the LVAD. On previous checkup visits to the hospital, the LVAD team would ask Rick to speak with veterans who were candidates for the device. Rick's talks with the veterans gave them an idea of what was possible with an LVAD. He'd explain how his quality of life had gotten back close to his normal routine. Rick would usually add the fact he missed being able to swim.

CHAPTER 20: Xmas

The holidays away from home are hard. Multiple holidays away from home are even harder. During Rick's stay a few years earlier with the LVAD surgery, we were at the hospital during the Easter Holiday. This stay in 2016 was at this point a four-month stay with no end in sight. Rick still had the LVAD and was still waiting for a donor's heart as an inpatient in the hospital. Auntie was doing well in the nursing facility back home. My daughter and her family were visiting our aunt as much as they could with their busy lives.

Guests of the Fisher House were coming and going during the holiday season. Most of the outcomes I saw were hopeful ones. I met a diverse group of people during this extended stay at the hospital. Some guests at the house stayed for no longer than a week and others for weeks on end. I was getting homesick but didn't want to leave. One of the important things about leaving the house was forfeiting the room if your leave was extended. I decided to wait a while longer before considering a visit home. Being with Rick on the holidays was important and I knew we both needed our spirits uplifted. Rick was still strong and getting his exercise every day in the hospital. On Sundays, we'd attend the church services in the hospital Chapel. I'd usually come over for the service and Rick would meet me at the Chapel. Following the service, I'd usually go back to the house to either prepare dinner or rest for my visit back at the hospital later in the afternoon.

Our twin grandbabies in our hometown were now close to eight months old. We'd only seen them for a little over three months of their young lives by the end of 2016. We were missing them terribly. I'd hope to see them at some point when I made the trip back home. I'd witness people in the house get visits from family members over the months I was at the house. I knew traveling with two babies and two older girls wouldn't be an easy drive for the parents. I'd hope they'd make the trip sometime during the holidays since Rick and I needed a morale booster during the long wait.

We were so happy to get a call that the kids would come for a visit a few days after Christmas. My daughter and her fiancé were able to get time off from work. The two school-age girls were out of school for the holidays, so the trip came at a perfect time. With assistance from the hospital social worker, I was able to coordinate accommodations for my family at the hospitality house.

The Fisher House management was always so helpful, and the holidays were not an exception. The manager knew my grandkids were coming and arranged to have gifts delivered before their visit. The toys were plenty and generous. The girls were so happy and surprised to get the gifts. We were so blessed to be taken care of so well. The visit with the girls and their parents lasted for several days. We were able to have a few meals with Rick at the hospital. One evening we all had dinner together in a private room at the hospital. We both enjoyed seeing all of them so much. The visit came at the right time and we were thankful that we got to see them. The holidays came and went so quickly but it was truly quality time. Rick told me how happy he was the kids were able to come and see us. We both knew the joy of having family present during those times.

New Year's Day of 2017 came on a Sunday. I remember getting up early to attend the hospital chapel services with Rick. We were excited about what the New Year would bring. The boost of finally seeing family was great medicine for us both.

Later in the month of January, I got ill. I felt it was bound to happen mostly because of the never-ending stress I was trying to keep under control. I had to go to the emergency room at a local hospital in another area of the city. Luckily, I was able to drive myself to the hospital. One of the house guests I'd become acquainted with came with me for support. The woman's husband was in ICU recovering from a critical condition. Unfortunately, as she waited with me, she got a call to go to the hospital because her husband was having complications. Friends of hers came to the emergency room to drive her back to the Veterans hospital. After my exam in the emergency room, I was given medications from the hospital pharmacy. Thankfully, I had insurance to cover the hospital bill except for a small copay amount. I stayed away from the hospital for a few days not wanting to get Rick sick. I was happy to find out the woman who went to the emergency room with me had good news after a few days. Her husband's condition was improving, and he was on the way to recovery. I remained thankful for the support I was given during my stay at the hospital.

After I'd fully recuperated from the emergency room visit, I knew it was time for a visit home. I needed checkups and follow-up care for conditions I'd neglected in the five months away from home. I scheduled a trip back home near the end of the month. I dreaded the long drive but knew it was necessary for lots of reasons. I wanted to see auntie and the family in addition to getting medical care. I was confident the trip back home on the road wouldn't be as rough as the trip down five months prior.

CHAPTER 21: On the Road Again

For my personal trip back home, I had more than a few things to pack. I'd accumulated lots of things during the five months stay. The bulk of the things I needed to take home were the gifts Rick received over the time he'd been at the hospital. There were veteran events every week at the hospital. On certain days there were local organizations that would host Bingo games. One of the popular prizes at the Bingo games were coupon books redeemable for items at the VA store. Some organizations would bring donated gifts of blankets, afghans, and books. I'd have to say the knitted and crocheted blankets were the most sought-after gifts by the veterans. Most of the items were beautifully handmade gifts. In addition to the Bingo games, organizations in the area would frequent different hospital units and deliver gifts to the veterans. I had a car trunk filled with items to take back home.

My road trip home was at the end of January on a Sunday. I wanted to avoid the weekday interstate heavy traffic as much as I could. The trip home was uneventful. I bought a prepared dinner when I was closer to home. Our refrigerator at home had already been cleared of old items by my future son-in-law. Coming home felt great. There's something about arriving in my hometown and seeing the skyline. The sight always gives me a twinge of happiness. The new townhome seemed strange and didn't feel like home yet. I was happy to relax in our living room the evening after I returned. I didn't do much unpacking at all. I'd only carried the necessary bags up from the car.

The next day was busy. I'd planned to visit my aunt in the nursing facility and go shopping for groceries. I had a couple of medical appointments I'd scheduled for the week as well. The visit to auntie the next day was a treat for both of us. It was the longest I'd been away from her in my entire life. Rick and I kept in touch with her by phone while we were away. The nurses at the facility kept me and my daughter, who's a registered nurse, updated on how our aunt was doing.

My first medical visit while at home was to my primary care doctor. The result was I needed to schedule a few diagnostic tests as soon as possible. I realized my stay was going to be a bit longer than the week I'd planned to stay. I was able to get my checkup and other annual visits I needed while I was home. Caregivers usually neglect themselves and suffer later. I honestly didn't think much about my health as much as I should've at the time. Once again, internal auto-pilot rules over everything. I was nervous about being away from Rick. My greatest hope was Rick would get the call about a donor heart being available for him. I'd have to get down to Richmond in hours to be there for him. I tried to arrange everything at home so that I could get back to Rick as soon as possible. The best-laid plans usually don't go as we plan them is what I've learned over time. It's a good saying, and it's true.

By mid-February, I was still at home coordinating things and sorting through months of mail. My daughter sent me mail regularly while we were in Richmond. After a while, it became too much, and I asked her to send only the bills. Our dining room table was full of magazines and flyers. I spent my evenings at home sifting through all the accumulated junk mail. I felt guilty not being with Rick for Valentine's Day. A good friend I'd known for years helped me coordinate a fruit arrangement for delivery to Rick at the hospital. The arrangement arrived on time and Rick loved it. After seeing auntie one last time, I was able to travel back to my home away from home on the following weekend.

The trip back was the same route I took six months prior. The awful trip alone where I'd had all the issues crossed my mind only a few times. I drove and stopped at familiar rest stops. I arrived back in Richmond and went directly to the hospital to see Rick. The reunion was great, and I could see he was as happy as I was that we were together again.

Being back at the Fisher House felt great. One of Rick's relatives living locally in Richmond was able to stand in for me so I wouldn't lose my room. We appreciated her generosity in taking time away from her busy life helping us. There was a turnover of guests at the house from week to week, so I saw new faces when I arrived back in the house. The Fisher House staff members were always helpful and became like an extended family of sorts. I was ready to get back to my daily routine.

By the following Friday, I'd been back in Richmond for six days. I decided to drive to a local shopping center in the early afternoon. My plan was to meet Rick for a late lunch in the hospital courtyard area. Staff and hospital patients alike would use the courtyard for lunch. I remember sitting in the car at the shopping center ready to drive out of the parking space when my cell phone rang. Rick was calling me. The first words out of his mouth when I answered the phone was, "Honey, they found a heart!" I felt as if my heart skipped a beat and I needed him to repeat what he said. I stepped on the brakes and put the car in park. Rick went on to say he wouldn't be outside to meet me because he was needed upstairs for lab work. A nurse had apparently come to the courtyard to get him for the testing. My husband asked me to drive safely and come to the hospital. I was excited and nervous driving back to the hospital. The moment we'd waited for all those past years had finally arrived!

I'd spoken with other family members of heart transplant recipients in the past. My understanding was when the call came a heart was available there would be some hours before the surgery would happen. I remembered hearing part of the process involved the heart being recovered and transported by the transplant team. I couldn't get there fast enough to be with my husband to experience the good news.

I arrived at the hospital and saw happy looks on the faces of the nursing unit's staff's as I walked past them. Everyone I saw smiled at me. It's truly a wonderful feeling when you realize so many people care. Rick was waiting for me in his room. He appeared much calmer than me. We made calls and lots of text messages for time's sake to family and friends. I personally requested special prayers from family and friends for the upcoming heart transplant surgery.

CHAPTER 22: The Blessing of Life

In the hours that passed after the news a donor's heart was available, we were given information about the expected time of the transplant surgery. Initially, it was scheduled for the wee hours of the morning. My plan was always to stay overnight in the hospital with Rick if the surgery happened overnight. I'd also planned to occupy my long wait during the surgery with baking at the Fisher House. I'd bought some quick cookie and muffin mixes to make for the houseguests. I'd planned to kill time and keep my mind occupied on other things until the surgery was completed. Again, the best-laid plans usually don't happen exactly as we want.

After rejoicing and informing the family of the donor's heart, I needed to get an overnight bag from my room. I'd told one of the houseguests I saw at the hospital of my good news. I traveled back to the Fisher House which stood no more than a quarter of a mile on the other side of the hospital property. Walking past the dining room area, I was greeted by a few of the houseguests with congratulations. The word of Rick's donor heart spread faster than I imagined. I thanked everyone and asked for prayers. I immediately headed back to the room to collect a bag, my electronic tablet, reading material, and a change of clothes.

There were a couple of hospital Chaplains we'd gotten acquainted with during our time at the hospital. We received visits from a couple of the Chaplains during that day. More than a few hospital staff members stopped by briefly to wish Rick well.

The medical staff told us that the heart would not arrive until hours later, but Rick would be taken down for prep several hours after midnight. Rick had a comfortable recliner in his hospital room. I planned to sleep on the recliner, or at least try with all the excitement and anticipation of the surgery.

The nurses on staff were helpful as always and made sure I was as comfortable as possible. Rick became acquainted with many people at the hospital. During that evening, people I hadn't met before stopped by the room to say hello and wish him good luck. My husband was fortunate to have so many people pulling for him. We knew how blessed we were.

I spent most of the evening talking with Rick in his room. We said prayers together and got a special visit from a Chaplain and his wife later in the evening. Rick was ready for what was to come. To me, my husband seemed fearless. *Let's light this candle* was his battle-cry of sorts. He was ready to face whatever came head-on. Amazingly, the surgery for the heart transplant was one day shy of exactly four years since the LVAD open-heart surgery. We saw the fact of the timing of the surgery as a great sign everything would work out along with our trust God was watching out for him.

Sometime around four in the morning, we were awakened by a nurse who told us it was time to prepare Rick to be taken down to the surgery area. We exchanged hugs and kisses and my husband told me, "I'll see you on the other side," as he'd done before the LVAD surgery four years earlier. Rick didn't look nervous on the outside as usual. If he was nervous, he didn't show it. My husband faced his challenges head-on. This life-saving surgery wasn't going to be any different in how he'd approach the situation. I love and admire his bravery.

After Rick left the room, I couldn't sleep anymore. I decided to stay close in hopes I'd get a status report on when the surgery began. I was told I'd hear something in a couple of hours or so. My plans for going back to the Fisher House to bake didn't happen. I was exhausted from the intermittent sleep in the recliner. After a few hours of not hearing anything, I asked one of the floor nurses if they'd knew if the surgery had begun. There wasn't a status update available in the system. I was told the transplant coordinator would be coming to see me soon. Back in the room, I calmed myself knowing God didn't take us this far to leave us alone. The coordinator eventually came to the room. She explained the wait was due to the heart arriving later than expected. Her promise to me was she'd keep me abreast of the surgery's progress by phone. The time was now about four hours from when Rick was rolled out of the room. As I expected, the day proved to be a long one.

Once the surgery was underway, the transplant coordinator informed me it was progressing well. I waited in his room and spent most of my time either watching television or using my electronic tablet to pass the time. Listening to music was also a good way to relax as I waited. When the surgery was completed many hours later, I got a call from the transplant coordinator. I was told Rick's new heart was in and was pumping on its own! I sent the text message to friends and family. The text read, *Thank You, Jesus! His new heart is in and pumping on its own. They are still doing closing procedures. Praise God!!"* Rick and I had waited so long for the day he'd get the donor's heart. Four years of blessings resulted in this wonderful gift!

It wasn't lost on us for a moment someone had to lose their life for Rick to get this miraculous gift of life. The heart came at the opportune time since Rick was healthy given his condition. My understanding was his chances were great for surviving the surgery because of his health status. We were encouraged he got the best heart available to match him. I asked about the heart donor. The only thing we were told was the heart came from a female in her twenties. Knowing a young woman lost her life made me sadder than I'd thought it would. I always knew we'd be grateful for a heart. One never knows how you'll feel about something unless you experience it. We prayed for the family who lost their loved one before and after the surgery. I asked if I could send a card to the family of the heart donor. We weren't given any location information on the donor's family. However, I was told I could compose a letter and card to the donor family. The transplant coordinator was responsible for getting our card and letter to the donor's family. We had no details of how or what happened to the heart donor. We were told the family wanted anonymity. Our hope was they'd know how appreciative we were for the life-saving gift.

We sent another card to the heart donor's family through the transplant coordinator around the Easter holiday. Since we didn't know of the religious beliefs of the donor family, our generic note indicated Rick was doing well and they were in our thoughts.

To be given the gift of life is the most precious of gifts. It wasn't until Rick's health crisis that I truly understood the importance of organ donation. I first signed up for organ donation at my state's department of motor vehicles many years before I met Rick. I must admit there were subsequent renewal periods where I didn't choose the organ donor status at the time of my license renewal, but never again. If more people chose organ donation, lives would be saved and long waits on transplant lists would be uncommon.

To register to become an organ donor in the United States, go to organdonor.gov or visit your state's department of motor vehicles office.

CHAPTER 23: The Invaluable Ones

One thing that kept Rick and me going was our faith in God. There's no way the entire process would have been tolerable if we didn't have our belief system. The support of our family and friends calling and sending text messages to say hello meant everything to us. Social media, namely Facebook, kept me connected with family and friends following our time away from home at the hospital. I had the iPad at the hospital during the day and used my laptop in the evenings when I was back in my room to keep connected.

Most of the people on my social media page were either family members, extended family, or friends. Social media was the quickest way to get the message out on prayer requests I had for Rick and the patients' families I'd met at the hospital. We both come from large families so individual updates to the family couldn't always happen. Phone calls were always returned to the people that didn't use social media. General updates of Rick's progress were shared on my Facebook page for friends and acquaintances. It was also important to us to find out how our family and friends were doing in their lives. We looked forward to seeing the people in our lives share pictures, videos, news stories, or a daily greeting. As I sifted through years of Facebook posts while writing this book, I'm touched at how those online expressions of love and support kept me going in those months in the hospital with Rick. Social media has many flaws, but it gave us a priceless lifeline to home.

I was happy to get calls wanting to keep tabs on me. The calls that asked me how *I* was doing never let me forget I was more than a spectator. I was fully immersed in the process of this transplant journey with Rick. Ultimately, I realized my husband would get the heart but we both shared the emotional experience. The calls from people asking if we needed anything were appreciated. Thankfully, we had everything we needed, but the gestures and offerings meant so much.

My adult daughter and her fiancé were our greatest support during the process. They both helped our aunt in the nursing home by taking care of her laundry and taking our grandkids to see her whenever possible. My aunt absolutely loved those visits and I'd hear the joy in her voice when I spoke to her on the phone after a visit from the kids. Taking care of our mail and sending it to me every month in bulk, was also a necessity and something my daughter was able to do for us. Seeing her take on the responsibility at home for us, was one of those precious gifts a parent hopes to get at some point in life – the affirmation that you've done *something* right as a parent.

My oldest sister lived a ten-hour drive away from Richmond. She'd call me often to check on Rick's condition and have long talks with me when she could. She always hoped she'd be well enough to come to Richmond and support me with a long visit while I stayed at the hospital with Rick. She was never well enough to make the trip, though. Rick and I traveled to visit my sister seven months after his transplant in 2017. I'm thankful we made the decision to make the long road trip to her home in Kentucky. My sister passed away less than two months before I began writing this book in 2018.

Since we can never know when we'll see someone for the last time, Rick and I agree we need to treasure our time with those we love. I'm glad I'd learned the lesson some years ago. My two other sisters offered words of support and love to carry us through the entire time away from home. A family can't be imitated or duplicated. It's everything. Family is more than blood relatives we find time after time.

One of my friends of over twenty-five years would call me practically every day to see how Rick and I were doing. She made those calls before we'd left home and while we were away. I'll never forget her faithfulness. We're still in touch and hope to be for the rest of our lives. If you're lucky enough to find a friend that supports you during good and bad times, you're fortunate.

There's another friend that I've known since childhood that would call periodically with encouraging words. Her conversations with me were uplifting as we often reminisced about our past experiences and the lessons we'd learned in life. I treasured her calls and how well she knew me. She was and remains a great friend to have.

There were people we became acquainted with throughout the medical process we now consider friends. There was yet another woman I became acquainted with in Richmond during Rick's LVAD surgery that was a great support to me. Her husband had his heart transplant during the time Rick received the LVAD. We became acquainted again when her husband needed care at the Richmond hospital as we waited for the heart transplant. Her husband recuperated, and she went back home to her home more than an hour's drive from Richmond. The same woman drove a long way to come down and sit with me on the evening of Rick's heart transplant. I was alone the entire day. Seeing her that evening and knowing she knew what I was going through was encouraging. She got dinner for both of us and just sat with me at the Fisher House for a long while. I assured her I was fine and wanted her to get back on the road. I was so thankful we crossed paths. She didn't have to extend her kindness, but she did at a time I needed it the most. I'll never forget her unselfishness.

There were a handful of other women I'd met at the Fisher House that made the time away from home easier to bare. One woman's husband that was a patient at the hospital, had a similar military background as Rick. After his discharge, the couple came to visit a few times during our long stay there. We continue to keep in touch.

Another of the invaluable people I met was the police officer that worked at the hospital. He gave words of encouragement to everyone in the Fisher House. He lifted my spirits and prayed for Rick and me often. He, along with the chaplains, medical staff, hospital staff, Fisher house staff, and patients' family members will forever hold a special place in our heart because they made our journey bearable.

CHAPTER 24: Critical Days

After Rick was out of the recovery area, I left his room to wait in the surgical waiting room. I was relieved to see the head cardiac surgeon walk into the waiting room. The surgeon told me the official news Rick got through the surgery and would be in the surgical intensive care unit for recovery. The surgeon's reputation preceded him. We were familiar with the renowned surgeon years before when Rick's LVAD was implanted. Now, this surgeon had performed the lifesaving heart transplant surgery on my husband. I'll be forever grateful to him, the other surgeons, and the medical staff involved in the heart transplant procedure.

Later in the evening on the day of the transplant surgery, it became time to clear Rick's belongings from his hospital room. The plan was for Rick to come back to the same surgical unit some days down the road when his condition stabilized. Of course, his hospital room couldn't remain unoccupied since bed space was at a premium. Rick had more than his share of personal items in the room since he'd been inpatient for over six months. Earlier in the day, I'd spent time packing Rick's things to take back to my room at the Fisher House. Some medical items were kept in storage on the floor at the hospital until Rick was transferred back to the acute care surgical unit. One of the charge nurses assisted me with getting the room cleared. I'd packed everything. I had to make two trips to the car to transport Rick's items.

The visit from my daughter and her family two months before the transplant was so uplifting. We had another visit from family during those first days of Rick's heart transplant surgery. Rick's sister was able to travel from another state to visit in the days following the transplant. He was still in critical condition and couldn't talk much. My sister-in-law's visit meant so much to both of us. She had a friend make the trip to Richmond with her. We appreciated the support which came right on time to give us encouragement.

Rick's quick recuperation from the heart transplant was surprising and wonderful. My husband opened his eyes within a day or so after the transplant. To his credit, he made an impact on the staff in his unit. Many of the staff members in his surgical unit passed by his ICU room to wave from the hallway at some point in the initial post-surgery days. Rick was up and walking in four days after the heart transplant. He initially walked around the ICU slowly but steadily. On the fifth day post-transplant, Rick surprised the staff in his old unit by walking down the hall to say hello. People talked about it in the days to come about how amazing it was that he was up so quickly. Another good thing was that he was eating a regular diet and feeling better.

After the heart transplant, there were biopsies needing to be done weekly for the first month to check for rejection of the heart. After that, the biopsy schedule changed over time. Rick's first heart biopsy was done about nine days after the transplant. The biopsy was done to check for rejection of the heart by sampling tissue. There's a grading scale. Without going into details above my layman knowledge, here's what I remember: A grade of zero "R" means no indication of rejection; and, on the other end of the scale, a grade of three "R" means severe rejection of the organ. Rick's first biopsy results were zero "R" and we were elated. It's the best feeling in the world. The next two biopsies of the heart had the same zero "R" rejection score and we were counting the days of Rick's discharge from the hospital.

CHAPTER 25: Wellness

Shortly before my husband's fourth biopsy was done something was awry. One of Rick's test results were showing signs of an infection and inflammation. I tried not to panic or show Rick my concern. I'd read about infections in the heart being serious and life-threatening depending on the type of infection. With Rick's immune system so compromised from the transplant surgery, everyone was concerned. The physicians initially ordered antibiotics to ward off infection. The infectious disease staff was consulted.

Rick and I had discussions with the infectious disease staff as well as the cardiac transplant team. The plan was to have Rick on the antibiotics for an extended period. Initially, the source of the infection was unknown. Sterilization and disinfection protocols during the previous procedures were checked. The result and plans were for the antibiotics to continue for at least six weeks.

Our stay was extended due to this *glitch* a bit longer than originally expected. I believe the extended stay was to make sure there were no other issues with whatever the infection results were showing. To this day, I'm not sure of the exact cause or origin of any infection Rick may have had at that time. What I do know, is that all signs of it were gone after a while. I know the power of prayer.

I had a lot of special *angels* in my corner during this time. At times when I wanted to run screaming for the hills, they were there to remind me of my blessings. I'm happy to say my meltdowns didn't happen often, but they did happen in a lowkey manner.

Rick was doing the hard part. I needed to keep it together for him. Friends and family reminded me of what they saw as my strength during our journey. I give the credit to God, for I'm nothing otherwise.

CHAPTER 26: After the Transplant

After a short while, Rick was transferred back to the acute care floor. I was so happy to be able to share his new chance at life with him. My husband was faithful to his exercise and physical therapy. He participated every day as ordered in helping to get his body strong and ready for discharge. Thankfully, his activity at the hospital keeping in shape helped him bounce back quickly from this major open-heart surgery.

Before and after the transplant Rick would save the VA store coupons from the Bingo games he'd won. Without my knowledge, he'd get a glass figurine gift from the store for me. He surprised me every so often with a new figurine as the months went passed. By the time he had the transplant, I had a collection of those glass figurines. I sat the figurines on the dresser in my bedroom at the Fisher House. The dresser chest sat against the wall near the foot of the bed. Every morning the figurines were the first things I saw when I opened my eyes. They were a pleasant reminder of the thoughtfulness of my husband.

The Easter service at the hospital chapel was special in many ways. Rick was finally strong enough to attend the services with me again. We were even more grateful than ever.

By the time the sixth heart biopsy was performed in late April of 2017, the plan was for us to head home in the next week or so. Rick's condition had stabilized. We were making definite plans to leave for home soon.

There were home health visits to set up with our hometown agencies. Of course, the hospital staff took care of coordinating the home care needed.

CHAPTER 27: Homebound

Spring had arrived, and Rick was doing well recuperating in the hospital. Birds were chirping outside my window and everything was right with the world, in my opinion.

Toward the end of our stay, Rick had a visit from two of his relatives who were now local to Richmond. One of the relatives was the person who helped with my spot at the Fisher House when I traveled back home earlier in the year. We all sat outside in the hospital courtyard and had lunch one sunny afternoon. It was a great time with my extended family.

The discharge date was finally set for the first week in May. Rick was discharged to the Fisher House. This day was to be the last night of our stay. I had my things packed and we transferred Rick's belongings from the hospital to my room at the Fisher House. There were weather reports of rain and thunderstorm warnings on the day we were set to leave. The storm caused damage and closed roads all around. We weren't too upset our departure was delayed. We wanted to be safe on the long drive back home. We prepared to leave the following morning. After looking at news and weather reports, we decided to drive the more scenic route back home. We drove northwest to avoid the damaging tornadoes and thunderstorms hitting the east coast at the time. Our safe arrival at home was over seven hours later.

CHAPTER 28: Home at Last

We got home and truly relaxed our minds for the first time in a while. A lot of time in those first weeks at home were spent organizing things in the house. We hadn't lived in the new place for long before we'd left for Richmond. The nine-month stay was well worth it since he came back with a new heart.

Rick still had the wound vacuum on his transplant incision to help with healing. A visiting home health nurse came to our home to care for his wound issues. Auntie was so happy to see

Rick walking into her room at the nursing facility on our first visit since we got back home. It was a joyous day.

Only a few weeks later, Rick's three-month post-transplant visit was scheduled. Since we stayed at the hospital a bit longer than expected, the scheduled checkup date came quickly. We needed to drive instead of fly to Richmond on this trip. There were personal items we'd left in Richmond due to a lack of space in the car when Rick was discharged a few weeks prior. There were also items shipped home prior to leaving the hospital. It's interesting the things one can accumulate without noticing. One of the friends I'd met at the Fisher House kept the items for me.

When June of 2017 had arrived, we made the decision (after lots of discussions) to move into another place. The townhome was spacious but there was an issue with the number of stairs for all three of us. Although Rick could do steps better than before, the steps were still an issue in these early days post-transplant. The steps would be difficult for auntie when we brought her back home as well. I wasn't a fan of steps either, with my issues. So, it was time to search for a new place. At the end of June, the second follow-up trip to Richmond was made. Rick had a good check-up and was doing as expected. We found a new place outside the city and close to the interstate leading to the city.

Around the time of the move to our new location in August of 2017, Rick wasn't feeling at all himself. He didn't have to do much physical work for the move since we hired professional movers again. We finished the move to the new place but still needed to clean the old townhome. As we were in the process of cleaning and sweeping in the old place, Rick told me he felt weak and needed to go to the hospital. Of course, I knew it had to be serious since we had a deadline to tidy up the townhome. The keys were due to be returned to the property's management office in another two days. Rick had proved to me to be someone who never stopped in the middle of a job or shirk his duties. Luckily the townhouse was minutes away from the Veterans hospital. After my husband's evaluation in the emergency room, the medical team consulted with the transplant team in Richmond. Rick had to be admitted to the hospital. His kidney function was seriously compromised. We were told he'd need to be in the hospital for a few days for treatment and observation.

Family members assured me what I already knew. Rick was a fighter and would pull through whatever was wrong. I remember being physically exhausted. Getting the large three-story townhome in shape for inspection by the property's management was required by the end of the weekend. To say it was a challenge with my health issues would be an understatement. However, God doesn't give you more than you can handle is a truth I've come to learn. I'll add the experience of the weekend as another character builder for myself. I considered calling around for help from friends or family members. In the end, I did the cleaning, vacuuming and sweeping of the three-floor townhouse on my own.

The few days in the hospital did wonders for Rick. His kidney functions bounced back to normal and he was discharged to home. On the morning of his discharge from the hospital, I put the final cleaning touches on the now-empty townhome. I picked Rick up from the hospital. He and I turned in the townhome keys before heading to our new place outside of town. In retrospect, I should have asked for help in cleaning the apartment, but I'm stubborn much like my husband. Another crisis averted.

Luckily, the six-month post-transplant follow-up was scheduled for the end of the month. I was eager to travel with Rick so he could be thoroughly checked out by the transplant team. The kidney function issues earlier in the month were concerning to us both. We made the trip by plane to Richmond in late August of 2017. Rick was doing much better by the end of the month and on his way to feeling normal again.

Normal is what you make it and our journey continues together.

EPILOGUE

As we finished the journey from LVAD to Transplant, our story will continue by the grace of God. We've learned many valuable lessons over the years together.

I would have to say one of the most valuable lessons we've learned was patience. We live in such a fast-paced world. Instant gratification is the normal way of life for most people. The technological age with all its bells and whistles makes it easy to take our inner treasures for granted. Waiting for blessings was difficult in the beginning, but we kept leaning on our faith to remind us of the important things in life. The first two years with the LVAD were the most difficult as we put our normal way of life on hold in anticipation of getting a new heart for Rick. We resumed our normal lives but proceeded with caution. We put off outings, and vacations in hopes a heart might be around the corner. The health crisis in 2014 made us know even more how fragile life can be at times. We were grateful to learn the lesson of patience.

Going through this journey also taught us both to be versatile. Our lives were in transition before the LVAD. Health concerns for us both changed our livelihood and way of life. We have lived the *for richer or for poorer* part of our vows as well as the *in sickness and in health part.* Those tests over time let us know we were better when we worked together.

Faith in God is the single most reason we're content in our lives today. We trusted the skills and knowledge of the surgeons and medical staff who helped us get through the journey. I thank the memory of our late parents for the groundwork of exposing us to God and his word. The seeds of faith were planted and nurtured as we lived our separate lives before we met. Every experience in our earlier lives led us to this journey together.

My husband was always more of a risk-taker than me. I've learned when you meet a person who touches your heart in the right way, fear won't break you. When you have someone by your side with unconditional loyalty, you have a great thing.

As I finish this book, we're enjoying our growing family. Grandchildren were born in recent years and our adult children are thriving in their lives.

Rick and I look forward to a future full of promise and only good things in our retirement. Whatever comes our way, I'm confident we'll handle it together and get it done.

Printed in Poland
by Amazon Fulfillment
Poland Sp. z o.o., Wrocław